Keep it Simple.   Make it Special.

Soups, Stews & Breads

Dedication

For everyone who simply loves a big bowl
of comforting soup!

Appreciation

Thank you to all of our Gooseberry Patch family & friends
who have shared their family-favorite recipes with us!

Gooseberry Patch
An imprint of Globe Pequot
246 Goose Lane • Guilford, CT 06437

www.gooseberrypatch.com
1·800·854·6673

U.S. to Metric Recipe Equivalents

Volume Measurements

1/4 teaspoon	1 mL
1/2 teaspoon	2 mL
1 teaspoon	5 mL
1 tablespoon = 3 teaspoons	15 mL
2 tablespoons = 1 fluid ounce	30 mL
1/4 cup	60 mL
1/3 cup	75 mL
1/2 cup = 4 fluid ounces	125 mL
1 cup = 8 fluid ounces	250 mL
2 cups = 1 pint =16 fluid ounces	500 mL
4 cups = 1 quart	1 L

Weights

1 ounce	30 g
4 ounces	120 g
8 ounces	225 g
16 ounces = 1 pound	450 g

Oven Temperatures

300° F	150° C
325° F	160° C
350° F	180° C
375° F	190° C
400° F	200° C
450° F	230° C

Baking Pan Sizes

Square

8x8x2 inches	2 L = 20x20x5 cm
9x9x2 inches	2.5 L = 23x23x5 cm

Rectangular

13x9x2 inches	3.5 L = 33x23x5 cm

Loaf

9x5x3 inches	2 L = 23x13x7 cm

Round

8x1-1/2 inches	1.2 L = 20x4 cm
9x1-1/2 inches	1.5 L = 23x4 cm

Recipe Abbreviations

t. = teaspoon	ltr. = liter
T. = tablespoon	oz. = ounce
c. = cup	lb. = pound
pt. = pint	doz. = dozen
qt. = quart	pkg. = package
gal. = gallon	env. = envelope

Kitchen Measurements

A pinch = 1/8 tablespoon	1 fluid ounce = 2 tablespoons
3 teaspoons = 1 tablespoon	4 fluid ounces = 1/2 cup
2 tablespoons = 1/8 cup	8 fluid ounces = 1 cup
4 tablespoons = 1/4 cup	16 fluid ounces = 1 pint
8 tablespoons = 1/2 cup	32 fluid ounces = 1 quart
16 tablespoons = 1 cup	16 ounces net weight = 1 pound
2 cups = 1 pint	
4 cups = 1 quart	
4 quarts = 1 gallon	

Table of Contents

Everyday Comfort Soups

Nothing warms you up quicker than a bowl of soup! Whether you're craving Hearty Vegetable Soup, Rainy-Day Tomato Soup or Fluffy Chicken & Dumplings, this chapter is full of the comforting soups you love. From Old-Fashioned Split Pea Soup to Grandpa Jo's Potato Soup, French Onion Soup to Chilled Gazpacho, look here to find all of your everyday favorites.

Marie's Vegetable Soup

North Woods Bean Soup✓
Sharon Demers, Dolores, CO

1/2 lb. turkey Kielbasa,✓
 halved lengthwise and
 sliced 1/2-inch thick
1 c. baby carrots, chopped
1 c. onion, chopped
2 cloves garlic, minced
4 c. chicken broth

1/2 t. Italian seasoning
1/2 t. pepper
2 15.8-oz. cans Great
 Northern beans, drained
 and rinsed
6-oz. pkg. baby spinach

Spray a Dutch oven with non-stick vegetable spray; heat
over medium-high heat. Add Kielbasa, carrots, onion
and garlic; sauté 3 minutes, stirring occasionally. Reduce
heat to medium; cook 5 minutes. Add broth, seasonings
and beans. Bring to a boil; reduce heat and simmer
5 minutes. Place 2 cups of soup in a blender or food
processor. Process until smooth; return processed soup
to pan. Simmer 5 more minutes; remove from heat. Add
spinach, stirring until it wilts. Serves 5.

Sent-to-Bed Tomato Soup✓
Margaret Welder, Madrid, IA

3 T. butter
1 stalk celery, diced
1/4 c. onion, minced
2 c. canned diced tomatoes
 with juice
1/4 t. baking soda
1 t. sugar

1 T. all-purpose flour
2-1/2 c. whole milk, ✓
 divided
2-1/2 t. salt, or to taste
1/4 t. pepper
Optional: minced fresh
 parsley

Melt butter in a saucepan over medium heat. Add celery
and onion; sauté until soft. Add tomatoes with juice;
bring to a boil. Add baking soda and sugar; stir down
the foam. In a jar with a tight lid, shake together flour
and one cup milk; add to mixture in saucepan. Stir in
remaining milk, salt and pepper; return to a boil. Cook,
stirring often, for about 2 minutes, until thickened.
Serve soup sprinkled with parsley, if desired. Makes 6
servings.

Marie's Vegetable Soup✓
Marie Needham, Columbus, OH

3 to 3-1/2 lb. beef chuck✓
 roast
1 head cabbage, quartered✓
2 onions, chopped
46-oz. can tomato juice
4 15-oz. cans mixed
 vegetables

28-oz. can diced tomatoes
6-oz. can tomato paste
salt and pepper to taste
Optional: hot pepper sauce
 to taste

Place roast in an ungreased large roasting pan; cover.
Bake at 325 degrees for 1-1/2 hours, until half done. Add
cabbage and onions to pan; add enough water to cover.
Bake an additional one to 1-1/2 hours, until roast is very
tender. Transfer contents of roasting pan to a large soup
pot; stir in remaining ingredients except hot sauce.
Simmer over medium-low heat for one to 1-1/2 hours.
At serving time, break up any large pieces of roast; add
pepper sauce, if desired. Makes about 10 servings.

Quick tip
To keep vegetables fresh and nutritious,
wrap them in paper towels and store them
in unsealed plastic bags in the refrigerator.

Brandi's Ultimate Tex-Mex Soup •
Brandi Howell, Owego, NY

1 T. olive oil
1 c. onion, diced
1 carrot, peeled and finely grated
1 T. ancho chili powder
1 T. garlic, minced
1-1/2 t. ground cumin
1 t. dried oregano
salt and pepper to taste
4 c. vegetable broth
13-oz. can chicken, drained

1 c. frozen corn, thawed
15-oz. can fire-roasted diced tomatoes
28-oz. can black beans, drained and rinsed
15-oz. can garbanzo beans, drained and rinsed
Garnish: sour cream, chopped fresh cilantro, lime wedges

Heat oil in a large stockpot over medium-high heat. Sauté onion in oil until golden and tender, 5 to 8 minutes. Add carrot and seasonings; cook one to 2 minutes. Add broth, chicken, corn, tomatoes with juice and beans. Cook over low heat for 25 to 30 minutes. Garnish as desired. Serves 6 to 8.

Brandi's Ultimate Tex-Mex Soup

Rainy-Day Tomato Soup
Rosie Sabo, Toledo, OH

2 T. olive oil
1 onion, thinly sliced
3 to 4 T. garlic, chopped
1 c. celery, chopped
1/2 c. carrot, peeled and cut into 2-inch sticks

28-oz. can crushed tomatoes
2-1/2 c. vegetable broth
2 t. dried basil
1 t. dried thyme

Heat oil in a Dutch oven over medium heat; add onion and garlic and sauté until onion is translucent. Add celery and carrot; cook 5 more minutes. Add remaining ingredients and bring to a boil. Reduce heat; cover and simmer 1-1/2 hours, or until thickened. Ladle soup into 4 bowls; top each serving evenly with Italian Croutons. Serves 4.

Italian Croutons:

1 loaf day-old bread, crusts removed
1/2 c. butter, melted

1 T. Italian seasoning

Cube bread and place in a large plastic zipping bag; set aside. Combine butter and seasoning; pour over bread. Mix well; arrange bread cubes on an ungreased baking sheet. Bake at 425 degrees for 10 minutes; turn bread cubes and bake 5 more minutes.

Quick tip

Add a tangy twist to bean soup by drizzling in some balsamic vinegar while it simmers.

Rainy-Day Tomato Soup

Chicken & Apple Wild Rice Soup

Tyson Ann Trecannelli, Gettysburg, PA

2 T. olive oil
2 carrots, peeled and chopped
1 onion, chopped
3 stalks celery, chopped
4 qts. chicken broth
4 boneless, skinless chicken breasts, cooked and shredded
1/3 c. wild rice, uncooked
2 t. dried tarragon
1 T. fresh parsley, chopped
salt and pepper to taste
3 Granny Smith apples, peeled, cored and chopped

Heat oil in a stockpot over medium heat. Sauté vegetables until tender, about 10 minutes. Add remaining ingredients except apples. Reduce heat to medium-low; cover and simmer for 45 minutes. Add apples and simmer for an additional 40 minutes, or until apples are tender and rice is cooked. Serves 8 to 10.

Chicken & Apple Wild Rice Soup

Italian Bean & Pasta Soup ✓

Mel Chencharick, Julian, PA

2 ham hocks
12 c. water
1 onion, chopped
1 c. celery, chopped
1 c. carrots, peeled and chopped
15.8-oz. can diced tomatoes
2 16-oz. cans navy beans, drained
2 T. dried Italian seasoning
2 c. ditalini pasta, uncooked

In a large Dutch oven over high heat, combine ham hocks, water, onion, celery and carrots. Bring to a boil. Reduce heat to low and simmer, uncovered, for one hour. Remove ham hocks and allow to cool. Remove meat from ham hocks, discarding skin, bones and fat. Return meat to Dutch oven; stir in tomatoes with liquid and remaining ingredients. Bring to a boil; reduce heat and simmer until pasta is tender, about 10 minutes. Serve immediately. Makes 10 to 12 servings.

French Onion Soup

Kristine Marumoto, Sandy, UT

6 onions, thinly sliced
1 T. oil
4 T. butter, divided
6 c. beef broth
salt and pepper to taste
1/2 c. Gruyère cheese, shredded and divided
1/2 c. shredded Swiss cheese, divided
1/2 c. grated Parmesan cheese, divided
6 slices French bread, toasted

Cook onions in oil and 2 tablespoons butter over low heat in a 3-quart saucepan until tender; add broth. Bring to a boil; reduce heat and simmer for 30 minutes. Remove from heat; season with salt and pepper. Ladle equally into 6 oven-safe serving bowls; sprinkle each bowl with equal amounts of each cheese. Arrange one bread slice on top of cheeses. Melt remaining butter; drizzle over bread slices. Place bowls on a baking sheet; bake at 425 degrees for 10 minutes. Broil until cheeses are golden; serve immediately. Makes 6 servings.

French Onion Soup

Summer Vegetable Soup

Summer Vegetable Soup ♪

Beth Stanton, Port Charlotte, FL

2 T. olive oil
1 c. leek, white and green parts, thinly sliced
1/2 c. carrot, peeled and grated
2 to 3 cloves garlic, minced
1 t. fresh oregano
4 c. chicken broth
14-1/2 oz. can diced tomatoes
15-1/2 oz. can Great Northern beans, drained, rinsed and divided
1 c. summer squash, chopped
1 c. zucchini, chopped
1/2 c. fresh or frozen corn
1/2 c. ditalini pasta, uncooked
1/2 t. kosher salt
1/2 t. pepper
2 c. fresh baby spinach
Garnish: basil pesto sauce, shredded Asiago cheese

Heat oil in a large Dutch oven over medium heat. Add leek, carrot, garlic and oregano. Cover and cook for 5 minutes, stirring occasionally. Add chicken broth and tomatoes with juice; bring to a boil. Reduce heat to low; simmer for 15 minutes. Place half of the beans in a bowl; mash with a fork. Add mashed beans, remaining beans, squash, zucchini, corn, uncooked pasta, salt and pepper to Dutch oven. Increase heat to medium; simmer for 10 minutes. Stir in spinach and cook for 3 more minutes, until wilted. To serve, ladle soup into bowls. Top each serving with a teaspoon of pesto and a tablespoon of cheese. Serves 4.

Quick tip

To remove drippings from soup, add a leaf of lettuce to the stockpot. Just remove the leaf after drippings are collected.

The Best Chicken Noodle Soup

The Best Chicken Noodle Soup ♪ p.20

Evelyn Belcher, Monroeton, PA

16-oz. pkg. thin egg noodles, uncooked
12 c. chicken broth
1-1/2 T. salt
1 t. poultry seasoning
1 c. celery, chopped
1 c. onion, chopped
1 c. carrot, peeled and chopped
1/3 c. cornstarch
1/4 c. cold water
4 c. cooked chicken, diced

Cook noodles according to package directions; drain and set aside. Meanwhile, combine broth, salt and poultry seasoning in a very large pot; bring to a boil over medium heat. Stir in vegetables; reduce heat, cover and simmer for 15 minutes, or until vegetables are tender. Combine cornstarch with cold water in a small bowl; gradually add to soup, stirring constantly until thickened. Stir in chicken and noodles; heat through, about 5 to 10 minutes. Serves 8 to 10.

Cheesy Vegetable Soup

Cheesy Vegetable Soup ◦

Belinda Gibson, Amarillo, TX

4 10-1/2 oz. cans chicken
  broth
2-1/2 c. potatoes, peeled
  and cubed
1 c. celery, chopped
1 c. onion, chopped
2-1/2 c. broccoli, chopped
2-1/2 c. cauliflower,
  chopped

2 10-3/4 oz. cans cream of
  chicken soup
16-oz. pkg. pasteurized
  process cheese spread,
  cubed
16-oz. pkg. pasteurized
  process Mexican cheese
  spread, cubed
1 lb. cooked ham, cubed

Combine broth, potatoes, celery and onion in a large
soup pot over medium heat. Simmer until vegetables are
tender, about 20 minutes. Add broccoli and cauliflower;
simmer an additional 10 minutes. Stir in soup, cheeses
and ham; simmer until cheeses melt and soup is heated
through. Serves 8 to 10.

GAZ.

Cool Summer Squash Soup ↓ P. 22 34

Pamela Jones, Fredericksburg, VA

1 clove garlic, minced
1/4 c. olive oil
1 c. sweet onion, chopped
1 to 2 yellow squash, sliced
1 to 2 zucchini, sliced
16-oz. can diced tomatoes
Optional: 1/2 spaghetti ✓
  squash

14-1/2 oz. can chicken or
  vegetable broth
1/4 t. dried oregano
1/4 t. dried parsley
salt and pepper to taste

celery bell pepper V8

In a large saucepan over medium heat, sauté garlic in oil.
Remove garlic; add onion and squash. Sauté until soft.
To a large soup pot, add squash mixture and remaining
ingredients. Simmer for 30 minutes; cool. Refrigerate
until ready to serve. Serves 4.

Spaghetti Squash Variation:
Microwave spaghetti squash on high setting, cut-side
down, for 8 minutes, or until easy to pierce. Remove
seeds; with a fork, scrape out pulp which will resemble
spaghetti. Cool; add pulp to soup mixture.

Quick tip

Is the soup or stew too salty? Just add a
peeled, raw potato and simmer. The potato
will absorb the excess salt.

Cool Summer Squash Soup

Beefy Hamburger Soup

Beefy Hamburger Soup

Chris Gravanda, Alden, NY

1 lb. ground beef
14-1/2 oz. can whole
  tomatoes, cut up
8-oz. can tomato sauce
6-oz. can tomato paste
1 c. onion, chopped
1 c. celery, chopped
1 c. carrots, peeled and
  sliced

1/3 c. pearled barley,
  uncooked
1/4 c. catsup
1 T. beef bouillon granules
2 t. seasoned salt
1 t. dried basil
salt and pepper to taste
1 bay leaf

In a large saucepan over medium heat, brown beef, stirring lightly to break up any large pieces. Drain; add tomatoes with juice and remaining ingredients; bring to a boil. Reduce heat to low. Cover and simmer for one hour, stirring occasionally. Remove bay leaf before serving. Makes 6 to 8 servings.

Midwestern Steakhouse Soup

Barbara Cooper, Orion, IL

1-1/2 lbs. boneless beef
  top sirloin steak, about
  1/2-inch thick, sliced into
  thin strips
2 T. oil
1 sweet onion, sliced
8-oz. pkg. sliced
  mushrooms
3 14-1/2 oz. cans beef
  broth

4 c. water
3 potatoes, peeled and cut
  into 1/2-inch cubes
2 t. Worcestershire sauce
Garnish: shredded
  Monterey Jack cheese,
  chopped fresh parsley

Brown steak strips in oil in a Dutch oven over medium heat for 5 minutes. Add onion and mushrooms; sauté until tender, about 5 to 10 minutes. Add remaining ingredients except garnish; simmer over low heat for 30 to 40 minutes. Transfer to a slow cooker. Cover and cook on low setting for up to 4 hours. Ladle into bowls and serve garnished with cheese and chopped parsley. Serves 6 to 8.

Midwestern Steakhouse Soup

Easy Hot Dog Soup

Dylan Bradshaw, Dublin, OH

3 potatoes, peeled and
  diced
1 onion, sliced
1 c. carrots, peeled
  and sliced
23-oz. can cream of
  mushroom soup

3 c. milk
4 hot dogs, sliced
1 c. frozen corn
1/2 t. garlic powder
salt and pepper to taste

Combine potatoes, onion and carrots in a large saucepan; cover with water. Cook over medium-high heat until nearly tender; drain. Whisk together soup and milk; add to cooked vegetables. Stir in hot dogs, corn and seasonings. Cook over medium-low heat until warmed through. Serves 4 to 6.

Country Comfort Chicken Soup

p.15 29

Fern Bruner, Palo Alto, CA

9 c. water

2 c. carrots, peeled and sliced

1 c. celery, chopped

2 T. garlic, minced

1-1/2 t. seasoned salt

1 t. dried parsley

1 t. poultry seasoning

1/2 t. salt

1/4 t. pepper

6 boneless, skinless chicken thighs

4 cubes chicken bouillon

5 c. fine egg noodles, uncooked

Place all ingredients except noodles in a large soup pot. Bring to a boil; cover, reduce heat and simmer until chicken and vegetables are tender, about one hour. Remove chicken; let cool slightly. Stir noodles into broth; simmer, uncovered, until done, about 5 minutes. While noodles are cooking, dice chicken and return to soup. Serves 8.

Quick tip

Place an apple into your bag of potatoes to keep them from budding.

Country Comfort Chicken Soup

Fluffy Chicken & Dumplings

Lori's Green Tomato Soup

Lori Rosenberg, University Heights, OH

2 T. olive oil

8 slices bacon

1-1/2 c. green onions, chopped

1 T. garlic, minced

1 bay leaf

1 t. salt

1/2 t. pepper

4 to 5 c. green tomatoes, chopped

1 c. chicken broth

2 c. water

Heat oil in a large pot over medium-high heat. Add bacon; cook until nearly crisp. Add green onions, garlic and bay leaf; cook until tender. Drain; stir in salt, pepper and tomatoes. Add broth and water. Bring to a boil; reduce heat to low. Partially cover and simmer for 35 minutes. Add more salt and pepper, if needed. Discard bay leaf before serving. Serves 4.

Fluffy Chicken & Dumplings

Angela Lengacher, Montgomery, IN

1 to 2 T. oil

1 c. celery, chopped

1 c. carrots, peeled and sliced

1 T. onion, chopped

49-oz. can chicken broth

10-3/4 oz. can cream of chicken soup

1/8 t. pepper

2 c. cooked chicken, chopped

1-2/3 c. biscuit baking mix

2/3 c. milk

Garnish: chopped fresh parsley

Heat oil in a Dutch oven over medium-high heat; sauté celery, carrots and onion 7 minutes, or until crisp-tender. Add broth, soup and pepper; bring to a boil. Reduce heat to low; stir in chicken and continue to simmer. To make dumplings, stir together baking mix and milk in a bowl. Drop by large spoonfuls into simmering broth. Cover and cook on low heat 15 minutes without lifting the lid, to allow dumplings to cook. Garnish as desired. Serves 6.

Kielbasa & Veggie Soup ↲

Karen Puchnick, Butler, PA

2 T. butter

1-lb. pkg. Kielbasa, diced

1 onion, chopped

1 c. celery, peeled and chopped

5 c. water

2 c. carrots, peeled and sliced

4 to 5 c. beef broth

10-3/4 oz. can tomato soup

2 to 3 T. catsup

2 T. vinegar

1 bay leaf

1/2 t. dried thyme

1 T. salt

3/4 t. pepper

2 c. potatoes, peeled and cubed

Heat butter in a Dutch oven over medium heat. Add Kielbasa, onion and celery; cook, stirring occasionally, until vegetables are tender. Add water and remaining ingredients except potatoes. Simmer, covered, over low heat one hour. Add potatoes and cook one more hour. Discard bay leaf. Serves 8 to 10.

Cajun Corn Soup ♪

Marie Stahl, Frankfort, IN

4 c. water	1 red pepper, chopped
6-oz. can tomato paste	2 c. frozen corn
1 t. salt	1/2 onion, chopped
1 t. pepper	4 cloves garlic, minced
1/2 t. cayenne pepper	1 T. oil
1 green pepper, chopped	1/2 lb. ground beef

Combine the first 8 ingredients in a large stockpot; heat over high heat to a boil. Reduce heat; simmer for 35 minutes. Sauté onion and garlic in oil in a 12" skillet until tender; add to soup. Brown ground beef in same skillet; drain. Stir into soup; simmer 10 additional minutes. Serves 6 to 8.

Cincy Navy Bean Soup ♪

Sandy Coffey, Cincinnati, OH

2 c. dried navy beans	1/2 to 1 bunch celery, stalks and tops, chopped
1 meaty ham bone	
12 c. water	1 clove garlic, minced
1/2 c. mashed potatoes — No	1/4 c. fresh parsley, finely chopped
1 to 1-1/2 c. onions, finely chopped	

Cover beans with water and soak overnight; drain. Put soaked beans, ham bone and fresh water in a soup kettle. Bring to a boil over medium heat; reduce heat to low. Cover and simmer for 2 hours, stirring occasionally. After 2 hours, stir in remaining ingredients. Simmer one more hour. Remove ham bone; dice meat and return to soup. Stir and serve. Makes 6 servings.

Cool Gazpacho Soup ♪

Sharon Tillman, Hampton, VA

p. 34   16
celery
radish
Tabasco

3 tomatoes, chopped	1 clove garlic, minced
2 cucumbers, peeled and chopped	32-oz. bottle cocktail vegetable juice
1/2 red onion, chopped	1 T. olive oil
1 green pepper, chopped	1 T. lemon juice
1 yellow pepper, chopped	

Combine all ingredients in a deep bowl; mix gently. Cover and refrigerate for at least 4 hours; serve chilled. Serves 6.

celery

Quick tip

A quick & easy way to crush tomatoes is to cut them in half, and with the cut side down, rub against a grater. In no time, just the peel is left in your hand.

Cajun Corn Soup

Sausage & Swiss Chard Soup

Sausage & Swiss Chard Soup

Phyllis Pierce, Greenfield, MA

6 c. water

2 bunches Swiss chard, sliced into 1-inch strips and stems discarded

4 T. olive oil, divided

6 cloves garlic, minced

1/2 t. red pepper flakes

1 T. tomato paste

4 to 6 links hot Italian pork sausage, casings removed and sliced 1-inch thick

2 carrots, peeled and diced

1 onion, chopped

2 stalks celery, chopped

28-oz. can diced tomatoes

2 15-oz. cans cannellini beans, drained and rinsed

2 14-oz. cans beef broth

2 14-oz. cans chicken broth

salt and pepper to taste

In a large stockpot over high heat, bring water to a boil. Add Swiss chard; cover and return to a boil. Reduce heat to medium-low and simmer for 15 minutes, or until tender. Drain chard in a colander; set aside. Meanwhile, in a large skillet, heat one tablespoon oil over medium-low heat. Add garlic and red pepper flakes. Cook, stirring constantly, for 2 minutes, or just until garlic is golden. Immediately stir in tomato paste; cook for one minute more. Add sausage and 2 tablespoons oil; cook until browned. Drain; remove sausage to a plate and set aside. Add remaining oil, carrots, onion and celery to pot. Cook over low heat until softened. Return sausage and chard to pot. Add tomatoes with juice and beans; stir well. Add broth, salt and pepper. Simmer for 30 minutes, stirring occasionally. Serves 8.

Quick tip

Hollow out a round loaf of pumpernickel bread to serve your soup for a quick and savory meal.

Mexican Albondigas Soup

Mexican Albondigas Soup

Sherry Sheehan, Phoenix, AZ

2 lbs. lean ground beef

1 c. Italian-seasoned dry bread crumbs

1 egg, beaten

Optional: 1/4 c. olive oil

3 stalks celery, sliced

1 green pepper, diced

1 c. carrots, peeled and diced

15-1/4 oz. can corn, drained

2 14-oz. cans beef broth

10-oz. can diced tomatoes with green chiles

4-oz. can diced green chiles

3 c. cooked rice

2 T. fresh cilantro, finely chopped

2 T. onion, minced

1 t. garlic powder

1 t. ground cumin

1 t. chili powder

1 t. salt

1/2 t. pepper

4 to 5 c. water

Combine ground beef, bread crumbs and egg; form into one-inch balls. Brown in a skillet over medium heat, adding oil if desired; drain. Place meatballs in a slow cooker and set aside. In a small saucepan, cover celery, green pepper and carrots with a little water. Cook until tender; add to slow cooker with remaining ingredients. Cover and cook on low setting for 3 to 4 hours. Serves 8.

Beef, Barley & Spinach Soup ♪

Alice Hardin, Antioch, CA

3/4 lb. lean ground beef
1 c. onion, chopped
14-1/2 oz. can diced tomatoes
1-1/2 c. carrots, peeled and thinly sliced
1/2 c. quick-cooking barley, uncooked
4 c. water
1-1/2 t. beef bouillon granules

1-1/2 t. dried thyme
1 t. dried oregano
1/2 t. garlic powder
1/8 t. salt
1/4 t. pepper
6-oz. pkg. fresh baby spinach

In a soup pot over medium heat, brown beef with onion, stirring to break up beef; drain. Stir in tomatoes with juice and remaining ingredients except spinach; bring to a boil over high heat. Reduce heat to low. Cover and simmer for 12 to 15 minutes, until barley and carrots are tender, stirring occasionally. Stir in spinach; simmer for several more minutes, until spinach starts to wilt. Makes 4 to 5 servings.

Quick tip

Chicken backs and wings are excellent for making delicious broth. Buy them fresh at the butcher's counter or save up unused ones in the freezer 'til you have enough for a quart of broth.

Mexican Soup

Carole Clark, Sterling Heights, MI

32-oz. container chicken or vegetable broth
2 14-1/2 oz. cans Mexican stewed tomatoes, chopped
1 c. cooked rice
1/4 c. fresh cilantro, chopped

6 canned chopped jalapeños, drained
Optional: 3 T. jalapeño juice
Garnish: shredded Cheddar cheese, sour cream, crushed tortilla chips

Add broth and tomatoes with juice to a soup pot over medium heat. Bring to a boil; reduce heat to low. Stir in rice, cilantro, jalapeños and jalapeño juice, if using. Simmer for about 10 minutes. Ladle into bowls; garnish as desired. Serves 4.

Kielbasa Kale Soup ♪

Robyn Burton, Maryville, TN

4 10-1/2 oz. cans chicken broth
4 10-1/2 oz. cans beef broth
8 c. kale, shredded
3 potatoes, peeled and cubed
1 onion, diced

3 carrots, sliced
2 stalks celery, diced
1 T. oil
14-1/2 oz. can diced tomatoes
1-1/2 lbs. Kielbasa, sliced
16-oz. can navy beans
hot pepper sauce to taste

Add first 4 ingredients to a large stockpot; cook over medium heat until potatoes are tender. Sauté onion, carrots and celery in oil until tender; add to broth mixture. Stir in tomatoes and Kielbasa; simmer for 30 minutes. Add beans; season with hot pepper sauce. Simmer until thoroughly heated through. Serves 10.

Kielbasa Kale Soup

Chicken Soup & Homemade Egg Noodles

Chicken Soup & Homemade Egg Noodles

Anita Gibson, Woodbury, MN

P. 15

5 to 6-lb. stewing chicken
6 c. chicken broth
4 carrots, peeled and diced
4 stalks celery, diced
1 T. fresh rosemary
16-oz. pkg. frozen mixed stew or soup vegetables
salt and pepper to taste
Optional: 1 t. lemon pepper

Place chicken in a large soup pot; add chicken broth, carrots, celery and rosemary. Bring to a boil over high heat; reduce heat to medium-low. Cover and simmer until chicken is tender, about 30 to 45 minutes. Remove chicken to a platter and let cool, reserving broth in pot. Chop chicken; return to broth. Return to a boil; reduce heat to low. Add frozen vegetables and seasonings. Simmer for one to 2 hours. Drop Egg Noodles into boiling soup; simmer for 30 minutes. Soup may be divided into several containers and frozen. Serves 6 to 8.

Egg Noodles: ✓

2 eggs, beaten
1/4 c. milk
THICK cut
1 t. salt
2 c. all-purpose flour

In a bowl, stir together eggs, milk and salt. Stir in enough flour to make a stiff, sticky dough. Gather dough into a ball. Roll out very thinly on a floured surface; let stand for 20 minutes. Roll up dough loosely; slice 1/4-inch thick. Let stand until ready to add to soup, or leave out to dry overnight. May store dried noodles in a container.

Quick tip

A pot of chicken soup and a cheery bouquet of posies are sure pick-me-ups for a friend who is feeling under the weather.

Old-Fashioned Tomato Soup

Old-Fashioned Tomato Soup

Fawn McKenzie, Wenatchee, WA

32-oz. can diced tomatoes
1 c. chicken broth
2 T. butter
2 T. sugar
1 T. onion, chopped
1/8 t. baking soda
2 c. light cream

Combine tomatoes with juice, broth, butter, sugar, onion and baking soda in a large stockpot. Simmer over low heat for one hour. Heat cream in a double boiler; add to hot tomato mixture. Blend well. Serves 4 to 6.

Old-Fashioned Split Pea Soup

Judy Steinbach, Rancho Cordova, CA

2-1/4 c. dried split peas
2-1/2 qts. water
2 ham bones
1-1/2 c. onion, chopped
1/4 t. garlic salt

1/4 t. dried marjoram
salt and pepper to taste
1 c. celery, chopped
1 c. carrots, peeled
  and chopped
1 t. dried parsley

Soak peas in water overnight; drain. Mix together peas, water, ham bones, onion, garlic salt, marjoram, salt and pepper in a stockpot. Bring to a boil over medium heat. Reduce heat and simmer for 2 hours; cut ham off of bones and return meat to soup. Stir in celery, carrots and parsley. Simmer for 45 minutes, or until vegetables are tender. Serves 8 to 10.

Stuffed Pepper Soup

Mary Lou Wincek, South Bend, IN

2 lbs. ground beef,
  browned and drained
8 c. water
28-oz. can diced tomatoes
28-oz. can tomato sauce
2 c. cooked long-grain rice

2 c. green peppers,
  chopped
2 cubes beef bouillon
1/4 c. brown sugar, packed
2 t. salt
1 t. pepper

Mix together all ingredients in a stockpot; bring to a boil over medium heat. Reduce heat and simmer for 30 to 40 minutes, until green peppers are tender. Serves 8 to 10.

Quick tip

When preparing soups that contain dairy products, easy does it! Cook them slowly over low heat...high heat causes milk and cream to curdle and separate.

Stuffed Pepper Soup

Chicken Minestrone

Hearty Vegetable Soup

Cheryl Hambleton, Delaware, OH

2 T. olive oil

1 onion, chopped

2 cloves garlic, minced

2 to 3 parsnips, peeled and
  thinly sliced

3 to 4 stalks celery, thinly
  sliced

3 carrots, peeled and
  thinly sliced

1 t. dried thyme

1/2 c. wild rice, uncooked

1/2 c. pearled barley,
  uncooked

7 to 8 c. beef broth

2 c. water

3 potatoes, peeled and
  cubed

1 tomato, diced

1 bunch fresh spinach,
  trimmed

salt and pepper to taste

Heat oil in a Dutch oven over medium heat. Add onion, garlic, parsnips, celery, carrots and thyme. Cook, stirring frequently, until vegetables soften. Stir in rice, barley, broth, water, potatoes and tomato. Cover and bring to a boil. Reduce heat to medium-low. Simmer, stirring occasionally, for one hour. Stir in remaining ingredients. Simmer for 2 to 3 minutes longer. Serves 6 to 8.

Hearty Vegetable Soup

Chicken Minestrone

Tara Pieron, Farmington, MI

5 10-1/2 oz. cans chicken
  broth

1 T. tomato paste

1-1/2 t. hot pepper sauce

1 t. dried oregano

1/2 t. dried rosemary

1-1/2 c. butternut squash,
  peeled and diced

1 T. butter

1 T. oil

1 onion, diced

3 tomatoes, chopped

1/2 lb. spinach, chopped

15-oz. can chickpeas

1 c. fresh basil, sliced

2 cloves garlic, minced

2 c. chicken, cooked and
  diced

6-oz. pkg. bowtie pasta,
  cooked

Bring broth to a boil in a large stockpot; add tomato paste, hot sauce, oregano and rosemary. Stir in squash and cook for 10 minutes; set aside. Heat butter and oil in a skillet; add onion and sauté for 4 minutes. Stir in tomatoes and heat for 3 minutes; spoon into broth mixture. Stir in spinach and chickpeas; cook for about 10 minutes. Stir in basil, garlic, chicken and pasta; heat through. Serves 6.

Quick tip

Seal in the flavor of onions and other soup veggies...simply sauté them in a little oil before adding broth and other ingredients.

Everyday Comfort Soups

Tomato Bisque
Sandy Spayer, Jeromesville, OH

2 c. chicken broth
14-1/2 oz. can whole
   tomatoes, broken up
1/2 c. celery, chopped
1/2 c. onion, chopped

3 tomatoes, chopped
3 T. butter
3 T. all-purpose flour
2 c. half-and-half
1 T. sugar

In a large saucepan over medium heat, combine broth, canned tomatoes, celery and onion; bring to a boil. Reduce heat; cover and simmer for 20 minutes. In a blender or food processor, process mixture in small batches until smooth. In the same saucepan, cook chopped tomatoes in butter for about 5 minutes; stir in flour. Add half-and-half; cook and stir over low heat until thickened. Stir in processed broth mixture and sugar; heat through without boiling. Makes 6 servings.

Tomato Bisque

Quick tip

Nothing perks up the flavor of tomato soup like fresh basil! Keep a pot of basil in the kitchen windowsill and just pinch off a few leaves whenever they're needed.

Chilled Gazpacho P. 22 16
Carrie O'Shea, Marina del Rey, CA

2 c. vegetable cocktail juice
3 lbs. ripe tomatoes,
   coarsely chopped
2 cucumbers, peeled and
   coarsely chopped
1 green pepper, coarsely
   chopped
 1/2 c. sweet onion, coarsely
   chopped

2 to 3 cloves garlic, minced
1/3 c. olive oil
3 T. white wine vinegar
salt and pepper to taste
Optional: hot pepper sauce
   to taste
Garnish: seasoned
   croutons

In a large bowl, combine tomato juice, vegetables and garlic. Working in batches, transfer mixture to a blender. Process to desired consistency; pour into a separate large bowl. Stir in olive oil and vinegar; season with salt, pepper and hot sauce, if desired. Cover and chill. Serve in chilled bowls, topped with croutons. Serves 6.

Chilled Gazpacho

Mom's Chicken-Veggie Soup

Tomato-Tortellini Soup◢

Diane Bailey, Red Lion, PA

1 T. margarine

3 cloves garlic, minced

3 10-1/2 oz. cans chicken broth

8-oz. pkg. cheese-filled tortellini, uncooked

1/4 c. grated Parmesan cheese

salt and pepper to taste

2/3 c. frozen chopped spinach, thawed and drained

14-1/2 oz. can Italian stewed tomatoes

1/2 c. tomato sauce

Melt margarine in a saucepan over medium heat; add garlic. Sauté for 2 minutes; stir in broth and tortellini. Bring to a boil; reduce heat. Mix in Parmesan cheese, salt and pepper; simmer until tortellini is tender. Stir in spinach, tomatoes with juice and tomato sauce; simmer for 5 minutes, or until heated through. Serves 8 to 10.

Tomato-Tortellini Soup

Thanksgiving Crab Soup•

Monica Vitkay, Bairdford, PA

6 c. water

30-oz. can beef broth

2-1/2 t. seafood seasoning

1/4 c. onion, chopped

16-oz. can whole tomatoes

20-oz. pkg. frozen mixed vegetables

5 c. potatoes, peeled and sliced

16-oz. can crabmeat

Combine water, broth, seasoning and onion in a stockpot and bring to a boil over medium-high heat. Reduce heat; add vegetables and simmer 1-1/2 hours. Add crabmeat and simmer 1-1/2 more hours. Serves 6 to 8.

Mom's Chicken-Veggie Soup◢

Marilyn Petersen, Boulder City, NV

1 to 2 T. olive oil

1/2 c. onion, chopped

2 T. garlic, chopped

1 c. carrots, peeled and diced

1 potato, peeled and diced

1 c. celery, diced

6 to 8 c. chicken broth

15-oz. can tomato sauce

1 c. boneless, skinless chicken, diced

3/4 c. frozen corn

1/2 c. frozen peas

2 t. dried parsley

1 t. lemon-pepper seasoning

1-1/2 c. wide egg noodles, uncooked

Heat oil in a large soup kettle over medium heat. Add onion and garlic; sauté for 3 to 5 minutes, until onion is translucent. Stir in carrots, potato and celery; sauté for an additional 8 to 10 minutes. Add remaining ingredients except noodles; simmer for 10 to 12 minutes. Add noodles and cook until tender, about 10 minutes. Makes 8 servings.

Chicken Broth from Scratch ♪

Christian Brown, Killeen, TX

3 to 4-lb. roasting chicken
2 T. olive oil
2 carrots, peeled and thickly sliced
2 stalks celery, thickly sliced
1 onion, halved
1 clove garlic, halved
2 qts. cold water
4 sprigs fresh parsley
4 sprigs fresh thyme
2 bay leaves
Optional: salt and pepper to taste

Place chicken in an ungreased roasting pan. Cover and roast at 350 degrees for about 1-1/2 hours, until juices run clear when pierced. Cool chicken and shred. Reserve pan drippings and bones; chicken meat may be reserved for another use. In a stockpot over medium heat, sauté vegetables in oil for 3 minutes. Add reserved bones, pan drippings, water and seasonings; simmer for one hour. Strain broth; season with salt and pepper, if desired. Makes about 8 cups.

Callie Coe's Chicken & Dumplings

Callie Coe's Chicken & Dumplings

Marilyn Meyers, Orange City, FL

3 to 4 lbs. bone-in chicken, cut up
3 qts. water
salt and pepper to taste
4 eggs, hard-boiled, peeled and chopped

Place chicken pieces in a large pan; add water, salt and pepper. Bring to a boil; reduce heat and simmer until tender and juices run clear when chicken is pierced with a fork, about one hour. Remove chicken, reserving broth in pan. Let chicken cool; remove meat, discarding bones, and return meat to chicken broth. Add chopped eggs. Bring broth to a boil and add Dumplings one batch at a time; stir well before adding each new batch. After adding last batch, cover and simmer until tender, about 20 minutes. Remove from heat; let stand a few minutes before serving. Serves 4 to 6.

Dumplings:

4 c. self-rising flour
1 to 1-1/4 c. warm water

Mix flour with enough water to make a dough that can be rolled out. Divide dough into 4 batches. Roll out each batch of dough 1/2-inch thick on a lightly floured surface; cut into strips.

Quick tip

Pick up a roast chicken or two from the deli...a quick start for recipes calling for cooked chicken.

Chicken Broth from Scratch

Nonnie's Italian Wedding Soup

Nonnie's Italian Wedding Soup ↓ p. 49

Liz Roaden, Miamisburg, OH

18 c. water
4 boneless, skinless ✓
  chicken breasts
1 yellow onion, peeled
1 c. celery, diced
1 c. carrot, peeled and
  diced
12 to 15 cubes chicken
  bouillon, or to taste

2 10-oz. pkgs. frozen
  chopped spinach, thawed
Optional: frozen mini
  meatballs, uncooked ✓
  acini de pepe or orzo
  pasta
Garnish: croutons

In a 6-quart stockpot, combine water, chicken and whole onion. Bring to a boil over medium-high heat. Reduce heat to medium and cook until chicken juices run clear, 10 to 15 minutes. Remove onion and discard. Remove chicken and shred; return to pot. Add celery and carrot; continue to simmer, uncovered, for 45 minutes. Stir in bouillon, spinach and meatballs, if using; simmer over low heat an additional 30 minutes. If desired, stir in pasta about 5 minutes before soup is done. Garnish with croutons. Makes about 25 servings.

Parmesan-Onion Soup

Pastina Soup ↓

Althea Paquette, South Attleboro, MA

1 meaty beef shank bone
6 carrots, peeled and sliced
6 stalks celery, diced
2 onions, chopped
3 tomatoes, diced

salt and pepper to taste
16-oz. pkg. orzo pasta,
  uncooked
Optional: grated Parmesan
  cheese

Cover beef shank bone with water in a Dutch oven; bring to a boil over medium heat. Add carrots, celery, onions, tomatoes, salt and pepper. Simmer over low heat 6 to 8 hours. Remove beef shank bone; cool and remove meat from bone. Add meat to soup; discard bone. In a separate pan, cook orzo 4 minutes; drain and add to soup. Simmer 5 more minutes. Sprinkle with Parmesan cheese, if desired. Serves 8.

Parmesan-Onion Soup ↓ p. 12

Linda Campbell, Huber Heights, OH

3 T. butter, melted
4 c. onions, thinly sliced
1/2 t. sugar
1 T. all-purpose flour
4 c. water

salt and pepper to taste
4 French bread slices,
  toasted
1/2 c. freshly grated
  Parmesan cheese

Combine butter, onions and sugar in a large saucepan; sauté 20 to 25 minutes, until onions are golden. Stir in flour; cook for 3 to 5 minutes. Add water and simmer, partially covered, for 30 minutes. Add salt and pepper, blending well. Fill 4 oven-proof bowls, arranged on a rimmed baking sheet, with soup; top each with a bread slice and sprinkle generously with Parmesan cheese. Bake at 400 degrees until cheese melts. Makes 4 servings.

Chicken, Lime & Tortilla Soup

Lisa Lankins, Mazatlán Mexico

3 to 3-1/2 lbs. chicken	1/4 c. corn
2 tomatoes, chopped	1/4 c. long-cooking rice, uncooked
1 jalapeño pepper, chopped	1 t. chopped green chiles
1/4 c. fresh cilantro, chopped	1 t. garlic, minced
juice of 3 limes	1/2 t. pepper
2 t. Worcestershire sauce	salt to taste
1 onion, chopped	Garnish: diced avocado, shredded Mexican-blend cheese, tortilla strips
1/2 c. red pepper, chopped	

Cover chicken with water in a stockpot. Bring to a boil over medium-high heat. Reduce heat to low; simmer about an hour, or until chicken is very tender and juices run clear when pierced. Remove chicken to a plate, reserving 4 cups broth in stockpot. Let chicken cool slightly. Add tomatoes, jalapeño, cilantro, lime juice and Worcestershire sauce to reserved broth; simmer 45 minutes. Meanwhile, chop half the chicken and set aside; reserve the rest for another recipe. Stir remaining ingredients except garnish into soup; simmer 20 more minutes. Stir in chopped chicken. Garnish individual servings as desired. Serves 6.

Quick tip

Add mild-flavored fresh herbs like marjoram and parsley to soups and stews near the end of cooking time...they won't lose their delicate flavor.

Chicken, Lime & Tortilla Soup

Caboosta Cabbage Soup✓

Janae Mallonee, Marlboro, MA

6 c. water	1-1/2 c. boneless pork, diced
28-oz. can crushed tomatoes	1 bay leaf
1/2 to 2/3 head cabbage, shredded	salt and pepper to taste

In a soup pot over medium heat, combine water, tomatoes with juice, cabbage, pork and bay leaf. Bring to a boil; reduce heat to low. Simmer for about 30 minutes, stirring occasionally, until pork is cooked and cabbage is tender. At serving time, discard bay leaf; season with salt and pepper. Makes 8 servings.

Caboosta Cabbage Soup

Tuscan Soup

Tuscan Soup

Jeanne Caia, Ontario, NY

2 T. olive oil
1/2 c. onion, peeled and diced
1 carrot, peeled and diced
1 redskin potato, diced
2 14-oz. cans chicken broth
1 c. water
1/4 t. dried marjoram
1/8 t. pepper
15-oz. can cannellini beans
2/3 c. tubetti or ditalini pasta, uncooked
1/2 head escarole, thinly sliced
Garnish: shredded Parmesan cheese

Heat oil in a large saucepan over medium-high heat. Add onion, carrot and potato; cook until lightly golden, about 5 minutes, stirring often. Add broth, water and seasonings; bring to a boil over high heat. Reduce heat to low. Cover and simmer for 10 minutes, or until vegetables are tender. Stir in undrained beans and uncooked pasta; bring to a boil over high heat. Reduce heat to low; cover and simmer for 15 minutes, or until pasta is tender, stirring occasionally. Stir in escarole; heat through. Top with Parmesan cheese. Makes 4 servings.

Spicy Vegetable Soup

Patricia Dammric, Saint Louis, MO

1 lb. ground beef
1 c. onion, chopped
1 c. celery, chopped
2 cloves garlic, minced
30-oz. jar chunky garden style spaghetti sauce
10-oz. can diced tomatoes with green chiles
10-oz. pkg. frozen mixed vegetables
2 potatoes, peeled and cubed
10-1/2 oz. can beef broth
2 c. water
1/2 t. chili powder
1 t. sugar
1 t. salt
1/2 t. pepper

salsa

Combine ground beef, onion, celery and garlic over medium heat in a stockpot; cook until beef is browned and onion tender. Drain; stir in remaining ingredients. Reduce heat and simmer for 1-1/2 hours to blend flavors. Serves 8 to 10.

Grandpa Jo's Potato Soup

Hope Davenport, Portland, TX

2 lbs. potatoes, peeled and diced
1/2 lb. carrots, peeled and diced
2 stalks celery, diced
1 onion, diced
4 c. water
12-oz. can evaporated milk
1/4 c. butter, sliced
seasoned salt with onion & garlic to taste
pepper to taste
8-oz. pkg. shredded Cheddar cheese
3 slices bacon, crisply ✓ cooked and crumbled

Combine vegetables and water in a stockpot over medium-high heat. Cook 15 to 20 minutes, until vegetables are fork-tender. Reduce heat to low; stir in evaporated milk, butter and seasonings. Heat through. Ladle into soup bowls; garnish with cheese and bacon. Serves 6.

Quick tip

Try using fat-free half-and-half in cream soup recipes. You'll get all the delicious richness without the calories of regular half-and-half.

Maple Autumn Squash Soup

Jo Ann

1 lb. butternut squash, peeled, cubed and boiled
1/2 c. butter, divided
1/4 c. maple syrup
3 T. brown sugar, packed
1 t. cinnamon
1/2 t. ground ginger
3 T. all-purpose flour
2 c. chicken broth
2 c. unsweetened applesauce
1 c. Granny Smith apples, peeled, cored and chopped
2 c. light cream
salt and pepper to taste

Combine squash with 4 tablespoons butter, syrup, brown sugar and spices; mash well and set aside. Melt remaining butter in a large pot over medium heat; add flour and cook for 3 minutes, stirring constantly. Blend in broth and cook until soup thickens. Stir in squash mixture, applesauce and apples. Cook over medium heat until warmed through, stirring often. Add cream and heat just until soup begins to bubble around the edges. Cool and refrigerate overnight. Reheat over medium heat until warmed through. Makes 6 to 8 servings.

Quick tip

Pre-warmed soup bowls are a thoughtful touch that's oh-so simple to do. Just place bowls in a 250-degree oven as you put the finishing touches on dinner.

Pasta e Fagioli

Pasta e Fagioli

Maddie Schaum, Mount Airy, MD

15-oz. can cannellini beans
2 T. olive oil
3 slices bacon, coarsely chopped
2 stalks celery, chopped
2 carrots, peeled and chopped
1 onion, chopped
2 cloves garlic, minced
3 14-1/2 oz. cans chicken broth
15-oz. can kidney beans, drained and rinsed
1 c. small shell pasta, uncooked
salt and pepper to taste
Garnish: 6 T. grated Parmesan cheese

Mash undrained cannellini beans with a fork in a bowl and set aside. Heat oil in a large saucepan over medium heat; add bacon and next 4 ingredients. Cook for 7 to 10 minutes, stirring occasionally, until bacon is crisp and vegetables are softened. Add broth, cannellini beans and kidney beans; bring to a boil over high heat. Stir pasta into soup. Reduce heat to medium. Cook, uncovered, for 6 to 8 minutes, stirring frequently, until pasta is tender. Add salt and pepper; top each serving with a tablespoon of cheese. Serves 6.

Maple Autumn Squash Soup

Fresh Tomato Soup

Fresh Tomato Soup
Joyce Penn, Columbus, OH

1 to 2 T. olive or canola oil
1 c. yellow onion, coarsely
  chopped
1 red pepper, coarsely
  chopped
2 T. onion soup mix

1 T. garlic, minced
6 tomatoes or 10 roma
  tomatoes, coarsely
  chopped
3/4 t. salt, or to taste
1/2 t. pepper, or to taste

Heat oil in a large saucepan over medium-low heat; add onion, red pepper, soup mix and garlic. Cook for 5 minutes, until onion is translucent. Stir in tomatoes, salt and pepper. Bring to a boil; reduce heat to low. Cover and simmer, stirring occasionally, for 20 minutes, or until tomatoes are very soft. Remove from heat. When cool enough to handle, transfer mixture in batches to a blender or food processor; process until soupy but still slightly chunky. May reheat and serve hot; serve at room temperature or chill before serving. Serves 4.

Cream of Potato Soup
Vickie

1 T. butter
1/2 c. green onions, sliced
2 c. chicken broth
1-1/2 lbs. new yellow
  potatoes, cubed

salt and pepper to taste
1-1/2 c. heavy cream
Garnish: additional sliced
  green onions

Melt butter in a large saucepan over medium-low heat. Add green onions; cook for one minute. Add broth, potatoes and seasonings; bring to a boil over high heat. Reduce heat to low. Cover and simmer until potatoes are tender, 15 to 20 minutes. Stir in cream; heat through without boiling. Garnish soup with additional onions. Makes 4 servings.

Traditional Wedding Soup ↓ p. 41
Marisa Adams, Manchester, CT

2 qts. chicken broth
4 ripe tomatoes, chopped
  and juice reserved
1 head escarole, chopped
1 T. dried basil

1 T. dried parsley
pepper to taste
Garnish: fresh parsley,
  grated Parmesan cheese

In a soup pot, bring broth to a boil; add remaining ingredients except Meatballs and garnish. Bring to a boil. Add Meatballs, a few at a time. Bring to a boil again; reduce heat and simmer until Meatballs are thoroughly cooked, about one hour. Garnish with fresh parsley and Parmesan cheese. Serves 6 to 8.

Meatballs:

1 lb. ground beef
1 egg
1 clove garlic, minced
1 T. dried parsley

1/4 c. bread crumbs
1/4 c. grated Parmesan
cheese

Combine all ingredients. Shape into 2-inch balls.

Quick tip

Add a creamy touch to milk-based soups... just substitute evaporated milk. It's easy to keep on hand since it needs no refrigeration...just keep a few cans on hand in the pantry.

Chapter 2

Hearty Chowders, Chilis & Stews

These soups will stick to your ribs! Cheeseburger Soup and Dijon Beef Stew will keep you full for hours. Looking for a creamy chowder? Try Tailgate Seafood Chowder or Cheesy Chicken Chowder. If you're new to making soup, why not try Beginner's Chili? It's sure to be a hit first time around.

Country Corn & Cheddar Chowder

Country Corn & Cheddar Chowder
Vicki Callahan, Saint Peters, MO

p.57
68
72
cream 103

6 ears corn, husked	2 t. ground cumin
3 T. butter, melted and divided	1 t. ground coriander
	1/2 t. cayenne pepper
1 c. onion, diced	1/2 t. salt
2 stalks celery, diced	8 c. chicken broth
1 leek, washed and diced	8-oz. pkg. shredded extra sharp Cheddar cheese
1 red pepper, diced	

Brush the ears of corn lightly with one tablespoon melted butter. Grill or broil corn until roasted on all sides, about 5 minutes. Slice off kernels, reserving the cobs. Add remaining butter to a large, heavy soup pot over medium heat. Add corn, remaining vegetables and seasonings; sauté until vegetables are soft but not browned. Pour in broth. Bring to a boil; reduce to a simmer and add reserved corn cobs. Simmer 40 to 45 minutes, stirring occasionally. Discard cobs; stir in cheese and serve immediately. Serves 8.

Pumpkin Chowder
Sandy Westendorp, Grand Rapids, MI

8-oz. pkg. bacon, diced	4 c. chicken broth
2 c. onions, chopped	1 c. half-and-half
2 t. curry powder	salt and pepper to taste
2 T. all-purpose flour	Garnish: toasted pumpkin seeds, sliced green onions
1-lb. pie pumpkin, peeled, seeded and chopped	
2 potatoes, peeled and cubed	

Cook bacon in a stockpot over medium heat for 5 minutes; add onion. Sauté for 10 minutes; add curry and flour, stirring until smooth and creamy, about 5 minutes. Add pumpkin, potatoes and broth; simmer until potatoes are tender, about 15 minutes. Pour in half-and-half; season with salt and pepper. Simmer for 5 minutes; do not boil. Spoon into serving bowls; garnish with toasted pumpkin seeds and sliced green onions. Serves 6.

Tailgate Seafood Chowder
Kathleen Brillinger, Norwich, NY

1/2 c. butter	2 19-oz. cans chunky clam chowder
1 lb. shrimp, peeled, cleaned and chopped	1/2 c. vermouth or chicken broth
3 8-oz. cans chopped clams, drained	pepper to taste
2 10-1/2 oz. cans she-crab soup	Garnish: fresh parsley, chopped

Melt butter in a large saucepan over medium heat; add shrimp to pan. Cook 2 to 3 minutes or until shrimp turn pink. Add remaining ingredients except parsley; cook until heated through. Garnish with fresh parsley. Serves 8 to 10.

Quick tip

Keep a bunch of fresh green parsley in the fridge, ready to add a little color and a taste of the garden to meals anytime. Simply place the bunch, stems down, in a glass of water and cover the top loosely with a plastic sandwich bag.

Wisconsin Cheese Soup

Kelly Simpson, Rapid City, SD

5 T. butter
2 stalks celery, chopped
1/2 green pepper, chopped
5 mushrooms, chopped
2 carrots, chopped
1 onion, chopped
1/2 c. cooked ham, diced
1/2 c. all-purpose flour
2 T. cornstarch
4 c. chicken broth
4 c. milk
1/2 t. paprika
1/2 t. mustard
16-oz. pkg. shredded sharp Cheddar cheese
1/4 to 1/2 t. cayenne pepper
salt and pepper to taste

Melt butter in a stockpot over medium heat; add vegetables and ham. Cook until vegetables are tender, about 10 minutes; stir in flour and cornstarch. Cook for 3 minutes; add broth and stir until thickened. Mix in remaining ingredients; cook until cheese is melted. Makes 8 to 10 servings.

Wisconsin Cheese Soup

Beginner's Chili

Denise Evans, Moosic, PA

1 lb. ground beef
1 onion, diced
1/2 green pepper, diced
1 clove garlic, diced
2 10-3/4 oz. cans tomato soup
6-oz. can tomato paste
3-1/4 c. water
1/2 t. chili powder
1/8 t. red pepper flakes
1/8 t. dried oregano
1/8 t. salt
1/8 t. pepper
1 bay leaf
Optional: 1/8 t. cayenne pepper
16-oz. can kidney beans
cooked rice and/or cornbread
Optional: sour cream, shredded Cheddar cheese

In a Dutch oven over medium heat, brown beef with onion, green pepper and garlic. Mash beef with a wooden spatula as finely as possible. Drain; stir in tomato soup, tomato paste, water and seasonings. Reduce heat to low. Cover and simmer for one hour, stirring occasionally. Lightly mash kidney beans with a fork in a bowl; stir into chili. Cook another 10 minutes. Discard bay leaf. Serve chili ladled over cooked rice or cornbread, or serve cornbread on the side. Top with a dollop of sour cream and a handful of cheese, if desired. Serves 4 to 6.

Quick tip

A quick & easy way to thicken bean soup...purée a cup of soup in a blender or even mash it in a bowl, then stir it back into the soup pot.

Beginner's Chili

Harvest Corn Chowder

Harvest Corn Chowder

Pat Habiger, Spearville, KS

53
P.68
72
103

1 onion, chopped
1 red pepper, chopped
1-1/2 t. garlic, minced
1/2 t. poultry seasoning
1/4 t. dried thyme
1 T. olive oil
4-oz. pkg. ham, chopped
2 potatoes, peeled and cut
into 1/2-inch cubes

2 c. water
1 T. chicken bouillon
granules
1-1/2 c. frozen corn,
thawed
1 c. chicken, cooked and
cubed
1-1/2 c. milk
3/4 c. half-and-half

In a saucepan, sauté onion, pepper, garlic, poultry seasoning and thyme in oil for 5 minutes; add ham. Cook for an additional 5 minutes; stir in potatoes, water and bouillon. Bring to a boil; reduce heat and simmer for 10 minutes. Mix in corn, chicken, milk and half-and-half; cook until warmed through. Serves 5.

Aztec Corn Chowder

Vickie

1/4 c. butter
3-1/2 c. corn
1 clove garlic, minced
1 c. chicken broth
2 c. milk
1 t. dried oregano
4-oz. can diced green
chiles

1 c. shredded Monterey
Jack cheese
salt to taste
Optional: chopped tomato,
chopped cilantro

Melt butter in a large saucepan over medium heat. Add corn and garlic; cook and stir until corn is heated through. Remove from heat. Place broth and 2 cups corn mixture into a blender. Cover and blend until smooth; stir into mixture in saucepan. Add milk, oregano and chiles and mix well; bring to a boil over medium heat, stirring constantly. Remove from heat; stir in cheese and salt to taste. Garnish with tomato and cilantro, if desired. Makes 4 to 6 servings.

Turnip Greens Stew

Turnip Greens Stew

Connie Hartings, Athens, OH

2 c. cooked ham, chopped
1 T. oil
3 c. chicken broth
1 t. sugar
1 t. seasoned pepper

2 16-oz. pkgs. frozen
chopped turnip greens
10-oz. pkg. frozen diced
onion, red and green
peppers and celery

Sauté ham in hot oil in a Dutch oven over medium-high heat 5 minutes or until lightly browned. Add broth and remaining ingredients; bring to a boil. Cover, reduce heat to low, and simmer, stirring occasionally, for 25 minutes. Serves 6 to 8.

Creamy White Chili

Janelle Dixon, Fernley, NV

1 T. oil
1 lb. boneless, skinless chicken breast, cubed
1 onion, chopped
14-oz. can chicken broth
2 15-1/2 oz. cans Great Northern beans, drained and rinsed
2 4-oz. cans chopped green chiles
1-1/2 t. garlic powder
1 t. salt
1 t. ground cumin
1/2 t. dried oregano
8-oz. container sour cream
1/2 pt. whipping cream
Garnish: crushed corn chips, shredded Monterey Jack cheese

Heat oil in a large skillet over medium heat; add chicken and onion. Sauté until chicken is cooked through; set aside. Combine broth, beans, chiles and seasonings in a large soup pot over medium-high heat; bring to a boil. Add chicken mixture; reduce heat and simmer for 30 minutes. Add sour cream and whipping cream; mix well. Garnish individual servings with chips and cheese. Serves 8.

Creamy White Chili

Chicken Pot-Pie Soup

Jennifer Clingan, Dayton, OH

1-1/2 c. butter
1-1/2 c. all-purpose flour
4 t. salt
1/2 t. pepper
4 c. half-and-half
6 c. seasoned chicken broth
6 boneless, skinless chicken breasts, cooked and cubed
5 to 6 potatoes, cubed and boiled
3 c. mixed vegetables

Puff Pastry

Melt butter in a large Dutch oven; whisk in flour, salt and pepper. Cook and stir over low heat until smooth and bubbly; remove from heat. Carefully whisk in half-and-half and broth; return to heat and bring to a slow boil. Reduce heat; add remaining ingredients, chopping into bite-size pieces if necessary. Simmer until vegetables are tender. Makes 8 to 10 servings.

Tomato-Ravioli Soup

Heather Quinn, Gilmer, TX

1 lb. ground beef
28-oz. can crushed tomatoes
6-oz. can tomato paste
2 c. water
1-1/2 c. onion, chopped
2 cloves garlic, minced
1/4 c. fresh parsley, chopped
3/4 t. dried basil
1/2 t. dried oregano
1/4 t. dried thyme
1/2 t. onion salt
1/2 t. salt
1/4 t. pepper
1/2 t. sugar
9-oz. pkg. frozen cheese ravioli, uncooked
1/4 c. grated Parmesan cheese

In a Dutch oven, brown beef over medium heat; drain. Stir in tomatoes, tomato paste, water, onion, garlic and seasonings. Bring to a boil. Reduce heat; cover and simmer 30 minutes. Cook ravioli according to package directions; drain. Add ravioli to soup and heat through. Stir in Parmesan cheese; serve immediately. Serves 6 to 8.

Chicken Pot-Pie Soup

Spicy Black-Eyed Pea Soup

Sheila Murray, Tehachapi, CA

4 slices bacon, diced
1 green pepper, chopped
1 onion, chopped
2 cloves garlic, minced
2 15-1/2 oz. cans
   black-eyed peas
2 14-1/2 oz. cans diced
   tomatoes
1 c. water

1-1/4 t. ground cumin
1-1/4 t. dry mustard
1 t. chili powder
1/2 t. curry powder
1/2 t. pepper
1/4 t. sugar
Garnish: shredded
   Monterey Jack cheese

In a large saucepan over medium heat, cook bacon until crisp. Remove bacon to paper towels to drain, reserving one tablespoon drippings in saucepan. In drippings, sauté green pepper, onion and garlic until tender. Add peas with liquid, tomatoes with juice, water and seasonings. Bring to a boil. Reduce heat, cover and simmer for 15 to 20 minutes. Garnish individual servings with reserved bacon and cheese. Serves 6 to 8.

Spicy Squash Soup

Spicy Squash Soup

Arden Regnier, East Moriches, NY

2 butternut squash, peeled,
   seeded and cubed
1 stalk celery, finely diced
1 jalapeño pepper, seeded
   and finely diced
1/2 onion, finely diced
2 c. chicken broth

12-oz. can evaporated milk
1/2 c. brown sugar, packed
1/2 c. water
salt and pepper to taste
ground cumin to taste

Place squash in a large saucepan and cover with water. Cook over medium-high heat until tender; drain. Mash squash and measure out 4 cups. Return 4 cups squash to saucepan over medium-low heat; stir in remaining ingredients except cumin. Simmer, covered, for 45 minutes. Cool slightly. Purée soup until smooth, adding to a blender in small batches. Return soup to saucepan over low heat just long enough to heat through; stir in cumin. Serves 6 to 8.

Quick tip

If canned beans don't agree with you, just drain and rinse them before using...you'll be washing away any "tinny" taste too.

Spicy Black-Eyed Pea Soup

Creamy Chicken & Gnocchi Soup

Creamy Chicken & Gnocchi Soup ◡

Annie Keplar, California, PA

1/2 onion, diced
1 stalk celery, diced
1/2 carrot, peeled and
　shredded
1 clove garlic, diced
1 T. olive oil
3 boneless, skinless
　chicken breasts, cooked
　and diced
4 c. chicken broth
2 c. half-and-half

1 T. dried thyme
1/8 t. salt
1/8 t. pepper
16-oz. pkg. gnocchi pasta, *diff!*
　uncooked
1/2 c. fresh spinach,
　chopped
1 T. cornstarch
2 T. cold water

In a large soup pot over medium heat, sauté onion, celery, carrot and garlic in oil until onion is translucent. Stir in chicken, chicken broth, half-and-half and seasonings; bring to a boil. Add gnocchi; cook for 4 minutes. Reduce heat to medium-low. Continue cooking for 10 minutes, stirring often. Add spinach; cook for one to 2 minutes, until spinach is wilted. In a cup, dissolve cornstarch in cold water. Return soup to boiling; add cornstarch mixture. Cook and stir until thickened. Serves 4.

South Carolina Gumbo

Rachel Reilly, Columbia, SC

1 T. olive oil
1 onion, chopped
1 stalk celery, sliced
1/2 green pepper, chopped
2 c. boneless, skinless
　chicken breasts, cubed
2 c. okra, chopped
2 14-1/2 oz. cans chicken
　broth

14-1/2 oz. can diced
　tomatoes
1 c. water
2 t. Cajun seasoning
1 t. salt
1/2 t. garlic powder
1/2 t. pepper
1 c. instant rice, uncooked

Heat oil in a stockpot over medium-high heat. Add onion, celery and green pepper; sauté until tender. Add chicken and remaining ingredients except rice; bring to a boil. Reduce heat and simmer, covered, 15 minutes, or until juices run clear when chicken is pierced. Add rice and simmer 15 more minutes. Serves 6 to 8.

Jambalaya ◡ *soup*

Patricia Perkins, Shenandoah, IA

2 T. butter
7-oz. pkg. chicken-flavored
　rice vermicelli mix
2-3/4 c. water
1/4 t. pepper *BROTH*
1/4 t. hot pepper sauce
1 T. dried, minced onion

1/4 c. celery, diced
1/4 c. green pepper, diced
2 c. cooked ham, diced
1 lb. cooked, peeled
　medium shrimp

Melt butter in a large saucepan over medium heat. Add rice vermicelli mix and sauté just until golden. Stir in remaining ingredients; reduce heat, cover and simmer for 15 minutes. Serves 4 to 6.

Curried Pumpkin Soup

Carol Allston-Stiles, Newark, DE

16-oz. pkg. sliced
  mushrooms
1/2 c. onion, chopped
2 T. butter
2 T. all-purpose flour
1 T. curry powder
3 c. chicken or vegetable
  broth

15-oz. can pumpkin
1 T. honey
1/8 t. nutmeg
salt and pepper to taste
1 c. whipping cream or
  evaporated milk
Garnish: sour cream,
  croutons

Sauté mushrooms and onion in butter in a large saucepan over medium heat until softened. Add flour and curry powder; cook 5 minutes, stirring constantly. Add broth, pumpkin, honey, nutmeg, salt and pepper. Reduce heat and simmer 15 minutes, stirring occasionally. Stir in cream or milk; heat through without boiling. Garnish servings with a dollop of sour cream and croutons. Serves 6.

Quick tip

Homemade soup always tastes even better if made a day ahead and refrigerated overnight. It's a snap to skim any fat too...it will solidify on the surface and can easily be lifted off.

Cream of Asparagus Soup ♪

Alice Livermore, Rochester, NY

4 c. chicken broth
pepper to taste
1 to 1-1/2 lbs. fresh
  asparagus, trimmed and
  broken into 1-inch pieces
1 onion, chopped
1/4 c. butter, sliced

4 c. half-and-half and/or
  milk
8-oz. pkg. American
  cheese, diced, or
  shredded Cheddar cheese
Optional: celery seed to
  taste

In a soup pot, bring chicken broth and pepper to a boil. Add asparagus and onion; reduce heat to medium-low. Cover and simmer until asparagus is very tender and falling apart. Add butter; stir until melted. Working in batches, process broth mixture in a blender. If a smoother texture is desired, strain broth mixture through a colander into another soup pot; press asparagus pulp through the colander. Return mixture to soup pot. Add half-and-half or milk, cheese and celery seed, if using. Cook and stir over medium-low heat until cheese is melted. Soup keeps well for several days in the refrigerator. Makes 6 to 8 servings.

Chili Con Carne

Catherine Matthews, Wise, VA

2 lbs. ground beef
1 onion, diced
2 14-1/2 oz. cans diced
  tomatoes
2 15-1/2 oz. cans dark or
  light kidney beans

2 T. chili powder
1 T. ground cumin
2 T. salt
1 T. pepper

Brown beef and onion in a large skillet over medium heat; drain. Add undrained tomatoes and beans; mix well and stir in seasonings. Bring to a boil. Reduce heat to low and simmer for 30 minutes, stirring occasionally. Add a little water if a thinner consistency is desired. Makes 8 servings.

Cream of Asparagus Soup

Tena's Delicious Gumbo

Black Beans & Vegetable Chili

Trisha Brady, Knoxville, TN

1 onion, coarsely chopped
1 T. oil
28-oz. can diced tomatoes
2/3 c. picante sauce
1-1/2 t. ground cumin
1 t. salt
1/2 t. dried basil
15-oz. can black beans, drained and rinsed
1 green pepper, cut into 3/4-inch pieces
1 red pepper, cut into 3/4-inch pieces
1 yellow squash or zucchini, cut into 1/2-inch pieces
hot cooked rice
Garnish: shredded Cheddar cheese, sour cream, chopped fresh cilantro
Optional: additional picante sauce

Sauté onion in oil in a Dutch oven over medium-high heat, stirring constantly, until tender. Add tomatoes with juice, picante sauce and seasonings; stir well. Bring to a boil; cover, reduce heat and simmer 5 minutes. Stir in beans, peppers and squash. Cover and cook over medium-low heat 25 minutes, or until vegetables are tender, stirring occasionally. To serve, ladle chili over hot cooked rice in individual bowls. Top each serving with cheese, sour cream and cilantro. Serve with additional picante sauce, if desired. Serves 4 to 6.

Tena's Delicious Gumbo

Tena Hammond Graham, Evans, GA

4 14-1/2 oz. cans chicken broth
7-oz. pkg. gumbo mix with rice
5 to 6 boneless, skinless chicken breasts, cooked and chopped
1 lb. Polish sausage, cut into bite-size pieces
2 10-oz. pkgs. frozen chopped okra
1 green pepper, chopped
1 red pepper, chopped
1 onion, chopped
pepper to taste
Cajun seasoning to taste
2 14-oz. pkgs. frozen popcorn shrimp

Combine all ingredients except shrimp in a large stockpot. Bring to a boil; reduce heat, cover and simmer for 25 minutes. Add shrimp; simmer an additional 5 to 10 minutes. Serves 10 to 12.

Quick tip

Save extra broth by freezing in an ice cube tray or muffin tin. Add the broth cubes when cooking rice or veggies...a real flavor boost.

Chicken Corn Chowder

Katie French, Portland, OR

1-1/2 c. milk

10-1/2 oz. can chicken broth

10-3/4 oz. can cream of chicken soup

10-3/4 oz. can cream of potato soup

1 to 2 10-oz. cans chicken, drained

1/3 c. green onion, chopped

11-oz. can sweet corn & diced peppers

4-oz. can chopped green chiles, drained

8-oz. pkg. shredded Cheddar cheese

Mix together all ingredients except cheese in a 6-quart saucepan. Cook over low heat, stirring frequently, for about 15 minutes, until heated through. Add cheese; stir until melted. Serves 6 to 8.

Quick tip

Need to feed a few extra guests? It's easy to stretch soup! Some quick-cooking add-ins are orzo pasta, ramen noodles, instant rice or canned beans. Simmer for just a few minutes until heated through.

Crawfish-Corn Chowder

Becky Garrett, Richardson, TX

12-oz. pkg. bacon, crisply cooked, crumbled and drippings reserved

2 c. potatoes, peeled and diced

1 c. onion, diced

2 T. butter

2 pts. half-and-half

2 16-oz. cans creamed corn

1 T. Cajun seasoning

Optional: 1 t. hot pepper sauce

1 lb. frozen crawfish tails or uncooked medium shrimp, peeled and cleaned

Place 1/4 cup reserved bacon drippings in a soup pot. Sauté potatoes and onion in drippings about 15 minutes or until golden. Stir in butter, half-and-half, corn, seasoning and hot pepper sauce, if desired. Add crumbled bacon to chowder. Cook over medium heat until potatoes are tender, about 20 to 30 minutes. Add crawfish or shrimp and simmer 15 to 20 more minutes; do not overcook shellfish. Serves 6 to 8.

No-Peek Stew

Mary Jo Urbaniak, Spokane, WA

2-1/2 lbs. stew beef, cubed

2 onions, quartered

4 stalks celery, chopped

4 potatoes, peeled and cubed

3 carrots, peeled and sliced

2 t. tapioca, uncooked

1 T. sugar

salt and pepper to taste

10-3/4 oz. can tomato soup

1-1/4 c. water

10-oz. pkg. frozen peas

Add ingredients in order listed to a Dutch oven; cover. Bake at 325 degrees for 4 hours. Serves 4.

No-Peek Stew

Chicken & Wild Rice Soup

Chicken & Wild Rice Soup ✓

Julia List, Lincoln, NE

2 c. cooked chicken, diced
6-oz. pkg. long-grain wild rice, cooked
2 10-3/4 oz. cans cream of mushroom soup
10-3/4 oz. can cream of celery soup
14-1/2 oz. can chicken broth
Optional: 2 T. sherry
1 carrot, peeled and shredded
4-oz. pkg. sliced mushrooms
1 pt. half-and-half

Combine all ingredients except half-and-half in a large stockpot; cook over medium heat until until vegetables are tender. Reduce heat to low; gradually stir in half-and-half, heating through without boiling, about 30 minutes. Stir often. Serves 6.

Chili with Corn Dumplings

Tanya Graham, Lawrenceville, GA

4-1/2 lbs. ground beef
2-1/4 c. onion, chopped
3 15-oz. cans corn, undrained and divided
3 14-1/2 oz. cans stewed tomatoes
3 15-oz. cans tomato sauce
1 T. hot pepper sauce
6 T. chili powder
1 T. garlic, minced
1-1/3 c. biscuit baking mix
2/3 c. cornmeal
2/3 c. milk
3 T. fresh cilantro, chopped

Brown ground beef and onion in a Dutch oven over medium heat; drain. Set aside 1-1/2 cups corn; stir remaining corn with liquid, tomatoes with juice, sauces, chili powder and garlic into beef mixture. Bring to a boil. Reduce heat; cover and simmer 15 minutes. Combine baking mix and cornmeal in a medium bowl; stir in milk, cilantro and reserved corn just until moistened. Drop dough by rounded tablespoonfuls onto simmering chili. Cook over low heat, uncovered, 15 minutes. Cover and cook 15 to 18 more minutes, or until dumplings are dry on top. Serves 10.

Chili with Corn Dumplings

Quick tip

Add big, fluffy dumplings to your favorite stew…easy! When the stew is nearly finished cooking, top with refrigerated biscuits and continue simmering 10 to 15 minutes, until done.

Red Barn Chowder

Red Barn Chowder ♪
Suzanne Pottker, Elgin, IL

1 lb. ground hot Italian sausage, crumbled

1 onion, chopped

3 stalks celery, chopped

1 green pepper, chopped

1 red pepper, chopped

2 zucchini, quartered and sliced

3 to 4 cloves garlic, chopped

28-oz. can stewed tomatoes

10-oz. can diced tomatoes with green chiles

6-oz. can tomato paste

1 c. water

2 t. dried basil

salt and pepper to taste

1 c. canned garbanzo beans, drained and rinsed

Combine sausage, onion, celery, peppers, zucchini and garlic in a large saucepan; sauté over medium heat until sausage is browned and vegetables are tender. Stir in tomatoes with juice, tomato paste, water, basil, salt and pepper; cook until heated through. Mix in garbanzo beans; heat through. Serves 8 to 10.

Colby Corn Chowder ♪ 68 59 m5
Vickie

6 potatoes, peeled and cubed

1 t. salt

1 onion, chopped

1/4 c. butter

2 14-3/4 oz. cans creamed corn

4 slices bacon, cooked and crisply crumbled

3 c. milk

8-oz. pkg. Colby cheese, cubed

Place potatoes in a soup pot; sprinkle with salt and cover with water. Bring to a boil over medium heat. Cover and simmer until potatoes are tender. Meanwhile, in a skillet over medium heat, sauté onion in butter until tender. Stir in corn and bacon; heat through. Drain potatoes; return to pot. Add milk and heat through over low heat. Stir in corn mixture and cheese; stir until cheese is melted. Serve immediately. Makes 12 to 14 servings.

Quick tip

Look for all kinds of fresh, ready-to-use veggies on your supermarket's salad bar. Buy just what you need...dinner preparation is a snap!

Colby Corn Chowder

Manhattan Clam Chowder

Manhattan Clam Chowder
Helen Burns, Raleigh, NC

1/2 lb. bacon, chopped
1 onion, sliced
2 cloves garlic, minced
28-oz. can whole tomatoes
2 6-1/2 oz. cans minced clams
8-oz. bottle clam juice
1 T. dried thyme
salt and pepper to taste
10-oz. pkg. frozen soup vegetables
1 to 2 potatoes, peeled and diced

Add bacon, onion and garlic to a skillet over medium heat; cook and stir until bacon is crisp and onion is tender. Drain; add to a slow cooker. Add remaining ingredients except frozen vegetables and potatoes. Cover and cook on high setting for 2 hours. Add vegetables and potatoes. Cover; reduce heat to low and cook for 3 to 4 hours longer, until vegetables are tender. Serves 4 to 6.

Ham & Corn Chowder
Molly Ebert, Columbus, IN

2 T. butter
1/2 c. onion, finely chopped
3 T. all-purpose flour
14-1/2 oz. can chicken broth
2 c. potatoes, peeled and diced
2 15-oz. cans corn
2 c. half-and-half
1-1/2 c. cooked ham, diced
2 T. fresh parsley, snipped

hard eggs soft.

Melt butter in a large saucepan over medium heat. Add onion and cook until tender, stirring frequently. Add flour; stir to make a paste. Slowly whisk in broth, stirring until smooth; add potatoes. Cover and cook for 10 minutes, or until potatoes are just tender. Stir in undrained corn and half-and-half. Reduce heat to low. Simmer, uncovered, for 6 to 8 minutes. Stir in ham and parsley; heat through but do not allow to boil. Makes 8 servings.

New England Fish Chowder

New England Fish Chowder
Maria Lemon, Boston, MA

1 T. oil
1/2 c. onion, chopped
2-1/2 c. potatoes, peeled and diced
1-1/2 c. boiling water
salt and pepper to taste
1 lb. frozen cod or haddock fillets, thawed and cut into large chunks
2 c. milk
1 T. butter
Garnish: fresh parsley sprigs

clam broth

Heat oil in a large saucepan over medium heat. Add onion; cook until tender. Add potatoes, water, salt and pepper. Reduce heat; cover and simmer 15 to 20 minutes, until potatoes are tender. Add fish; simmer about 5 minutes, until fish flakes easily with a fork. Add milk and butter just before serving; heat through. Garnish servings with parsley sprigs. Serves 6.

Cheesy Chicken Chowder

Grandma Logsdon's Beef Stew
Teresa Amert, Upper Sandusky, OH

1-1/2 lbs. beef round steak, cut into bite-size pieces
1 T. oil
1/4 c. all-purpose flour
2-1/2 c. water, divided
1 c. tomato juice or sauce
5 potatoes, peeled and quartered
1 onion, sliced
2 carrots, peeled and chopped
1 stalk celery, chopped
1/2 c. peas
Optional: 1/2 c. green beans
salt and pepper to taste

In a large soup pot over medium heat, brown beef in oil. Drain; sprinkle with flour and mix in. Slowly add 1/4 cup water; stir well. Add tomato juice or sauce and an additional 1/4 cup water; stir together and bring to a boil. Stir in remaining water; add remaining ingredients. Cook, partially covered over low heat, until beef and vegetables are tender, about one hour. Ladle into rimmed dinner plates. Serves 4.

Quick tip

Crunchy tortilla strips are a tasty addition to southwestern-style soups. Cut tortillas into strips, then deep-fry quickly. Drain, then sprinkle on top of soup.

Cheesy Chicken Chowder
Ann Cass, Danielsville, GA

32-oz. can chicken broth
2 c. potatoes, peeled and diced
1 c. carrots, peeled and thinly sliced
1/2 c. onion, diced
1 t. salt
1/4 t. pepper
1/4 c. butter
1/3 c. all-purpose flour
2 c. milk
2 c. shredded sharp Cheddar cheese
2 c. cooked chicken, chopped
15-oz. can corn, drained

Bring broth to a simmer in a large stockpot over medium heat. Add vegetables, salt and pepper; cook until tender. Melt butter in a separate saucepan; add flour and whisk until smooth. Gradually add milk to butter mixture; cook and stir until mixture starts to thicken. Add to stockpot; stir until well mixed. Add cheese; stir until melted. Add chicken and corn. Simmer until heated through, about 3 to 5 minutes. Serves 6.

Grandma Logsdon's Beef Stew

Ghostly White Chili

Ghostly White Chili

Wanda Sims, Madison, IN

9 c. chicken broth

1 onion, chopped

10-oz. can diced tomatoes with green chiles

4-1/2 oz. can chopped green chiles

2 15-oz. cans Great Northern beans

2 t. dried cumin

2 t. dried oregano

1/4 t. ground cloves

3 c. boneless, skinless chicken breasts, cooked and diced

Garnish: shredded Monterey Jack cheese, sour cream

Mix together all ingredients except chicken and garnish in a large saucepan and simmer over low heat for 1-1/2 hours. Add chicken; cook until heated through. Spoon into serving bowls; garnish with cheese and sour cream. Serves 8 to 10.

Tea Room Squash Soup

Charmie Fisher, Fontana, CA

6 to 8 crookneck yellow squash, sliced

2 onions, chopped

1 t. garlic powder

1/2 c. butter

1/4 t. baking soda

16-oz. pkg. pasteurized process cheese spread, cubed

2 c. half-and-half

salt to taste

Combine squash and onions in a large saucepan; cover with water. Cook over medium heat until vegetables are fork-tender. Drain most of the liquid. Working in batches, purée mixture in a food processor until smooth; transfer to a large saucepan. Add remaining ingredients. Heat through over medium-low heat, until cheese is melted. Serve soup in small bowls. Makes 8 servings.

Cape Cod Clam Chowder

Cape Cod Clam Chowder

Robin Cornett, Spring Hill, FL

2 10-3/4 oz. cans New England clam chowder

10-3/4 oz. can cream of celery soup

10-3/4 oz. can cream of potato soup

2 pts. half-and-half

3 potatoes, peeled and diced

salt and pepper to taste

Optional: chopped fresh chives

Combine soups and half-and-half in a large stockpot. Cook over medium-low heat until heated through, stirring often. Set aside over low heat. Boil potatoes in water for about 10 minutes; drain and add to soup mixture. Cook over medium heat until potatoes are tender. Add salt and pepper to taste. Garnish with chives, if desired. Serves 6 to 8.

Down-Home Soup Beans

Claire Bertram, Lexington, KY

1 lb. dried Great Northern
  or pinto beans
12 c. water
1 to 1-1/2 c. cooked ham,
  diced
1 onion, diced

Optional: 1 c. baby
  carrots, sliced
1 clove garlic, minced
1/4 t. red pepper flakes
1/2 t. salt
1 t. pepper

Combine all ingredients in a large Dutch oven; bring to a boil. Reduce heat and simmer, stirring occasionally, until beans are very tender and beginning to pop, 1-1/2 to 2 hours. Add a little more water while simmering, if needed, to make sure beans are just covered. Remove from heat. Transfer 2 cups of beans to a bowl and coarsely mash with a fork. Return mashed beans to pot; stir to combine and heat through. Serves 8.

One-Pot Spicy Black Bean Chili

Lisanne Miller, Canton, MS

1 onion, chopped
2 t. garlic, minced
2 t. olive oil
3 15-oz. cans black beans,
  drained and rinsed
16-oz. pkg. frozen corn
10-oz. can diced tomatoes
  with green chiles
1/2 c. water

1-1/2 t. taco seasoning mix
7-oz. can chipotle chiles in
  adobo sauce
1 T. rice vinegar
1/4 c. fresh cilantro,
  chopped
Garnish: sour cream, salsa,
  fresh cilantro sprigs

In a saucepan over medium heat, sauté onion and garlic in oil for 5 to 7 minutes, until softened. Add beans, corn, tomatoes, water and taco seasoning. Bring to a boil; reduce heat to low and simmer for about 15 minutes, stirring occasionally. Combine chiles in sauce and vinegar in a blender; process until puréed. Stir chile mixture and cilantro into chili; heat through. Garnish servings as desired. Makes 4 servings.

One-Pot Spicy Black Bean Chili

Quick tip

Canned yellow or white hominy makes a tasty, filling addition to any southwestern-style soup. Simply drain, rinse and add to the soup pot.

Down-Home Soup Beans

Julieanne's Chowder

Julieanne's Chowder

Julieanne Young, Millinocket, ME

1/2 c. salt pork or bacon, diced
1 onion, diced
2 stalks celery, diced
4 potatoes, peeled and diced
8-oz. bottle clam juice
1-1/2 lbs. haddock, rinsed
5-oz. can evaporated milk
pepper to taste
1-1/2 t. dried parsley
1 T. butter

Sauté salt pork or bacon in a Dutch oven until crisply cooked; remove and set aside. Add the onion and celery to the Dutch oven and sauté until translucent; remove and set aside. Place potatoes and clam juice in the Dutch oven. Cover with water; bring to a boil, reduce heat and simmer until soft. Add haddock; return to a boil, reduce heat and simmer for 5 minutes. Stir in milk, onion mixture, pepper and parsley. Heat through; stir in butter and heat until butter is melted. To serve, ladle potatoes and liquid into bowls. Add a piece of fish to each bowl; garnish with reserved salt pork or bacon. Serves 4.

Tortilla Stew

Donna Cannon, Tulsa, OK

2 15-1/2 oz. cans hominy
2 15-1/2 oz. cans chili beans
2 14-1/2 oz. cans Mexican-style stewed tomatoes
2 11-oz. cans sweet corn & diced peppers
2 10-oz. cans diced tomatoes with green chiles
2 10-oz. cans chicken, drained
2 1-oz. pkgs. ranch salad dressing mix
1/2 onion, chopped
salt and pepper to taste
tortilla chips
Garnish: shredded cheese, sour cream, guacamole

Stir together undrained vegetables and remaining ingredients except chips and garnish in a large stockpot. Simmer over medium heat for 30 minutes. Place a handful of chips into individual serving bowls; spoon stew over chips. Garnish as desired. Serves 8 to 10.

Tortilla Stew

Autumn Chili Soup

Debra Collins, Gaylesville, AL

1 lb. ground beef
14-1/2 oz. can can diced tomatoes
15-1/2 oz. can kidney beans, drained and rinsed
15-oz. can corn, drained
10-oz. can diced tomatoes and green chiles, drained
2 c. water
1-oz. pkg. taco seasoning mix

Brown beef in a large stockpot over medium heat; drain. Stir in undrained tomatoes and remaining ingredients; bring to a boil. Reduce heat to low. Simmer, uncovered, for 15 to 20 minutes, stirring occasionally. Makes 6 servings.

Hearty Chowders, Chilis & Stews

Christmas Eve Soup 🌶

Jessica Heimbaugh, Gilbert, IA

2 c. potatoes, peeled and
    diced
1/2 c. carrot, peeled and
    diced
1/2 c. celery, chopped
1/4 c. onion, chopped
2 c. water
1-1/2 t. salt

1/4 t. pepper
1 c. cooked ham, cubed
1/4 c. margarine
1/4 c. all-purpose flour
2 c. milk
8-oz. pkg. shredded
    Cheddar cheese

Combine vegetables, water, salt and pepper in a large soup pot. Bring to a boil over medium heat. Reduce heat; cover and simmer until vegetables are tender. Stir in ham; set aside. In a separate saucepan, melt margarine; stir in flour until smooth. Gradually add milk; bring to a boil. Cook and stir for 2 minutes, until thickened. Stir in cheese until melted; add to vegetable mixture and heat through. Serves 8.

Quick tip

Top bowls of hot soup with plain or cheesy popcorn instead of croutons for a crunchy surprise.

Christmas Eve Soup

Yankee Chili

Kathleen Peters, Arlington, TX

2 lbs. ground beef
1 onion, chopped
1 green pepper, chopped
28-oz. can whole tomatoes
15-1/2 oz. can kidney
    beans
10-3/4 oz. can tomato soup

2 T. chili powder
2 t. dried cumin
2 t. paprika
Optional: shredded
    cheese, chopped onions,
    crackers, bread & butter

In a Dutch oven over medium-high heat, brown beef with onion and green pepper for 10 to 12 minutes. Drain; add tomatoes with juice, beans with juice, soup and seasonings. Stir to combine and bring to a boil. Turn heat to medium-low and simmer for one to 2 hours. Stir occasionally, breaking up whole tomatoes with the back of your spoon. Garnish as desired. Serves 6.

Yankee Chili

Grandma Hallie's Spicy Chili

Hearty Sausage Soup

Wendy Dye, Monroe, NC

1 T. olive oil
3 lbs. Kielbasa sausage, cut into bite-size pieces
3 onions, diced
3 cloves garlic, minced
3 16-oz. cans kidney beans, drained and rinsed
3 14-1/2 oz. cans diced tomatoes, drained
14-1/2 oz. can beef broth
1/2 c. long-cooking rice, uncooked
0.67-oz. pkg. fresh basil, chopped
1 t. Italian seasoning
1 t. dried oregano
1 t. dried parsley

Heat oil in a large stockpot over medium heat. Add Kielbasa, onions and garlic. Cook until golden; drain. Add remaining ingredients; bring to a boil over medium-high heat. Reduce heat to low; simmer for 1-1/2 hours, stirring occasionally. Makes 8 to 10 servings.

Hearty Sausage Soup

Tortilla Chicken Stew

Ethel Carpenter, Helena, MT

2 10-oz. cans chicken, drained
2 15-1/2 oz. cans chili beans
15-1/2 oz. can pinto beans, drained and rinsed
2 14-1/2 oz. cans Mexican-style stewed tomatoes
2 11-oz. cans sweet corn & diced peppers
2 10-oz. cans diced tomatoes with green chiles
2 1-oz. pkgs. ranch salad dressing mix
1/2 onion, chopped
salt and pepper to taste
Garnish: corn or tortilla chips, shredded cheese, sour cream, guacamole

Stir together all ingredients except garnish in a large stockpot. Simmer over medium heat for 30 minutes. Spoon individual portions over corn or tortilla chips. Garnish as desired with shredded cheese, sour cream and guacamole. Serves 8 to 10.

Grandma Hallie's Spicy Chili

Ashley Hull, Virden, IL

2 lbs. ground beef
1/4 c. dried, minced onion
2 t. salt
2 10-3/4 oz. cans tomato soup
2 16-oz. cans kidney beans
2-1/2 c. water
1 t. Worcestershire sauce
2 T. butter, sliced
3 T. chili powder

In a large soup pot, brown beef over medium heat; drain. Add remaining ingredients; reduce heat to medium-low. Simmer for 45 minutes, stirring occasionally. Makes 8 to 10 servings.

Curried Harvest Bisque
Kathy Grashoff, Fort Wayne, IN

1 lb. butternut squash, peeled and cut into 1-inch cubes	3 T. curry powder
	3/4 c. half-and-half
	3 T. lime juice
5 c. chicken broth	1/2 t. salt
1/4 c. butter	1/4 t. white pepper
1/4 c. all-purpose flour	

Combine squash and broth in a heavy 4-quart stockpot. Cook over medium heat about 15 minutes, until squash is tender. Using a slotted spoon, transfer squash to a blender or food processor; process until smooth. Stir broth into puréed squash; set aside. Melt butter in stockpot; stir in flour and curry powder. Cook over medium heat, stirring until smooth. Add squash mixture; increase heat to medium-high and stir until soup thickens slightly. Reduce heat to low. Add half-and-half and remaining ingredients; heat thorough (do not boil). Serves 6.

Curried Harvest Bisque

Quick tip

It's best to remove bay leaves before serving your soup or stew. Tuck them into a metal tea ball that can hang on the side of the soup pot...easy to retrieve when done.

Kielbasa Bean Pot
Sharon Crider, Lebanon, MO

2 16-oz. cans pork & beans	1/4 c. water
1 lb. Kielbasa sausage, sliced	2 t. brown sugar, packed
	1 T. mustard
1-1/2 oz. pkg. onion soup mix	Garnish: sliced green onions
1/3 c. catsup	

Combine all ingredients except garnish in a 2-quart casserole dish. Bake, uncovered, at 350 degrees for one hour. Sprinkle servings with sliced green onions. Serves 6 to 8.

Kielbasa Bean Pot

Hunting Cabin Chili

Hunting Cabin Chili

Wendy West Hickey, Wexford, PA

2 to 3 lbs. ground beef
1 onion, chopped
1 green pepper, chopped
16-oz. jar salsa
30-oz. can light red kidney beans, drained
3 15-1/2 oz. cans dark red kidney beans, drained
28-oz. can whole tomatoes
1/8 t. hot pepper sauce
salt to taste

Brown beef in a large soup pot over medium heat; drain. Add remaining ingredients to pot. If needed, add enough water to just cover ingredients. Bring to a boil. Reduce to low; cover and simmer for 2 to 3 hours, until thickened. Serves 8 to 10.

Dijon Beef Stew

Amy Butcher, Columbus, GA

1-1/2 lbs. stew beef, cubed
1/4 c. all-purpose flour
2 T. oil
salt and pepper to taste
2 14-1/2 oz. cans diced tomatoes with garlic and onion
14-1/2 oz. can beef broth
4 carrots, peeled and cut into bite-size pieces
2 potatoes, peeled and cut into bite-size pieces
3/4 t. dried thyme
2 T. Dijon mustard

Combine beef and flour in a large plastic zipping bag; toss to coat evenly. Brown beef in oil over medium-high heat in a stockpot. Sprinkle to taste with salt and pepper. Add remaining ingredients except mustard. Bring to a boil; reduce heat. Cover and simmer for one hour, or until beef is tender. Blend in mustard. Serves 6 to 8.

Curry Butternut & Apple Soup

Carla Slajchert, Tampa, FL

1 butternut squash, halved and seeded
2 t. butter, divided
salt and pepper to taste
2 Granny Smith apples, peeled, halved and cored
2 c. chicken broth
1 t. garlic powder
1 t. onion powder
1 t. curry powder
1/2 c. sour cream
1 T. lime juice

Place squash halves cut-side up on a baking sheet. Add one teaspoon butter to each half; season with salt and pepper. Place apples next to squash on pan. Bake at 400 degrees for 30 to 45 minutes, until fork-tender. Scoop out squash pulp with a spoon. In a large saucepan, combine squash pulp, apples, broth and seasonings. Bring to a simmer over medium heat. Simmer for about 10 minutes, until heated through. Meanwhile, stir together sour cream and lime juice; set aside. Purée soup in batches in a blender until smooth; reheat soup, if desired. Serve in soup bowls, topped with dollops of sour cream mixture. Makes 4 to 6 servings.

Quick tip

Cheesy quesadillas are quick and filling paired with soup. Sprinkle a flour tortilla with shredded cheese, top with another tortilla and toast lightly in a skillet until the cheese melts. Cut into wedges and serve with salsa.

Down-East Fish Chowder
Lynda Robson, Boston, MA

3 to 4 slices bacon
1 c. onion, chopped
3 to 4 potatoes, peeled and cubed
1/2 t. garlic powder
1/2 t. dried oregano
1/2 t. paprika

2 12-oz. cans evaporated milk
1 lb. cod or other white fish, cut into chunks
salt and pepper to taste
oyster crackers

In a Dutch oven over medium-high heat, cook bacon until crisp. Remove bacon to a paper towel, reserving drippings in pan. Add onion, potatoes and seasonings to drippings; cook and stir until onion is tender. Stir in evaporated milk; bring just to a boil. Reduce heat to low; cover and simmer for 20 minutes, stirring occasionally. Add fish; cover and simmer an additional 10 minutes, until fish flakes easily with a fork and potatoes are tender. Season with salt and pepper; garnish with crisp bacon. Serve with oyster crackers. Serves 6.

Pop's Harvest Chili
Odell Underwood, Mount Hope, WV

1 lb. ground beef
1/2 lb. ground pork sausage
1/4 c. green onions, chopped
1-oz. pkg. chili seasoning mix
1/2 c. yellow, red or orange pepper, diced

1 c. sliced mushrooms
15-1/2 oz. can Great Northern or pinto beans
14-1/2 oz. can lima beans
14-1/2 oz. can Italian-seasoned diced tomatoes

In a heavy Dutch oven over medium heat, combine beef, sausage and green onions. Sauté until browned; drain. Stir in seasoning mix, pepper, mushrooms and undrained beans and tomatoes. Simmer over low heat until vegetables are soft, about 10 minutes. Add enough water to cover ingredients, or to desired consistency. Simmer for 20 to 30 minutes, stirring occasionally. Serves 6 to 8.

Oven Beef Stew
Alice Monaghan, Saint Joseph, MO

1-1/2 lbs. stew beef, cubed
5 carrots, peeled and sliced
1 c. celery, chopped
2 onions, sliced
1 potato, peeled and chopped

2 14-1/2 oz. cans stewed tomatoes
1/2 c. soft bread crumbs
2 t. salt
3 T. instant tapioca, uncooked

Place beef, carrots, celery, onions and potato in a bowl. Combine remaining ingredients and add to beef mixture; blend well. Place in a greased 2-1/2 quart Dutch oven. Cover and bake at 325 degrees for 4 hours. Serves 6.

Quick tip

A casual potluck soup supper is perfect for catching up with family & friends. Everyone is sure to discover new favorites, so be sure to have each person bring along extra copies of his or her recipe to share.

Oven Beef Stew

Wash-Day Stew

Wash-Day Stew
Sandra Crook, Jacksonville, FL

1-1/2 lbs. stew beef, cubed
1/2 c. frozen mixed
  vegetables, thawed
1 c. water
28-oz. can stewed
  tomatoes
1 T. salt

2 T. sugar
1/2 c. celery, sliced
1/2 c. onion, chopped
2 c. potatoes, peeled and
  diced
1 c. carrot, peeled and
  diced

Place all ingredients into a 6-quart Dutch oven. Cover and bake at 350 degrees for 4 hours. Stir stew; cover and bake for an additional 3 hours. May also be prepared in a slow cooker on low setting for 8 hours. Serves 6 to 8.

Easy as A, B, Seafood Bisque ♪
Weda Mosellie, Phillipsburg, NJ

6-oz. can crabmeat,
  drained
10-oz. pkg. imitation
  lobster, flaked
6-oz. can tiny shrimp,
  drained
1/2 c. plus 3 T. butter,
  divided
1 onion, chopped
1 carrot, peeled and
  chopped

1 stalk celery, chopped
14-oz. can chicken broth
Optional: 1/2 c. white wine
1 T. tomato paste
3 c. half-and-half
1/2 c. all-purpose flour
salt and pepper to taste
Garnish: fresh chives,
  chopped

Combine crabmeat, lobster and shrimp in a bowl; set aside. Melt 3 tablespoons butter in a large Dutch oven and sauté onion, carrot and celery about 3 minutes. Add chicken broth, seafood and wine, if desired. Bring to a boil; reduce heat and simmer. Stir in tomato paste and half-and-half. Melt remaining butter and blend with flour in a small bowl; stir into soup. Add salt and pepper. Simmer over low heat, stirring occasionally, 40 minutes. Garnish with chives, if desired. Serves 4 to 6.

Cheeseburger Soup ♪
Lacy Mayfield, Earth, TX

p.138

2 c. potatoes, peeled and
  cubed
2 carrots, peeled and
  grated
1 onion, chopped
1 jalapeño pepper, seeded
  and chopped
1 clove garlic, minced
1-1/2 c. water
1 T. beef bouillon granules
1/2 t. salt
1 lb. ground beef, browned
  and drained

2-1/2 c. milk, divided
3 T. all-purpose flour
8-oz. pkg. pasteurized
  process cheese spread,
  cubed
Optional: 1/4 to 1 t.
  cayenne pepper
Garnish: 1/2 lb. bacon,
  crisply cooked and
  crumbled

Combine first 8 ingredients in a large saucepan; bring to a boil over medium heat. Reduce heat and simmer until potatoes are tender. Stir in beef and 2 cups milk. Whisk together flour and remaining milk in a small bowl until smooth; gradually whisk into soup. Bring to a boil; cook 2 minutes or until thick and bubbly, stirring constantly. Reduce heat; add cheese and stir until melted. Add cayenne pepper, if desired. Garnish with bacon. Serves 6 to 8.

Quick tip

Busy day ahead? Use a slow cooker to make soup...it practically cooks itself! Soup that simmers for 2 hours on the stovetop can usually be cooked on the low setting for 6 to 8 hours or even longer.

Chapter 7

Slow-Cooker Soups

There's nothing like the aroma of slow-cooking soup, and these recipes are perfect for all-day cooking. Hearty Meatball Stew, Ham & Lentil Soup, Buffalo Chicken Stew...what's not to love? Toss the ingredients in your slow cooker in the morning and by dinnertime you've got a tasty meal just waiting to be enjoyed.

Yummy Pizza Soup

Yummy Pizza Soup

Karen Hart, Franklin, TN

1 lb. ground beef
1 lb. ground Italian pork
  sausage
1 onion, chopped
8-oz. pkg. sliced pepperoni
28-oz. can crushed
  tomatoes
2 8-oz. cans tomato sauce
4-1/4 oz. can chopped
  black olives, drained

3 cubes chicken bouillon
2 c. water
1 t. dried oregano
1 t. dried basil
1 t. garlic powder
16-oz. pkg. medium shell
  pasta, uncooked
Garnish: 2 c. shredded
  mozzarella cheese

In a large skillet over medium heat, brown beef, sausage and onion; drain. Add beef mixture and remaining ingredients except pasta and cheese to a slow cooker. Cover and cook on low setting for 4 to 6 hours. About 15 minutes before serving, cook pasta according to package directions; drain. Serve soup ladled over pasta in individual bowls; top with cheese. Serves 8 to 10.

Coal Miners' Stew

Christine Jaworski, Riverside, RI

4 potatoes, peeled and
  sliced
16-oz. pkg. Kielbasa
  sausage, sliced
2 14-1/2 oz. cans green
  beans, drained
1 onion, chopped

2 cloves garlic, minced
2 10-3/4 oz. cans cream of
  mushroom soup
1 to 2 c. shredded Cheddar
  cheese

Layer all ingredients in a slow cooker in the order given. Cover and cook on low setting for 6 to 8 hours. Makes 6 servings.

Mary's Easy Chicken Chili

Brenda Hager, Nancy, KY

2 10-oz. cans chicken
  breast, drained and
  flaked
4 c. chicken broth
3 15-oz. cans pinto beans,
  kidney beans, black
  beans, Great Northern
  beans or a combination,
  drained and rinsed

16-oz. jar medium salsa
Garnish: sour cream,
  shredded Cheddar
  cheese, chopped fresh
  chives, tortilla strips

Combine all ingredients except garnish in a slow cooker. Cover and cook on low setting for 2 hours, or until hot and bubbly. Serve garnished with desired toppings. Makes 6 to 8 servings.

3-Meat Slow-Cooker Chili

Beth Goblirsch, Minneapolis, MN

1 lb. ground beef, browned
  and drained
1 lb. ground pork sausage,
  browned and drained
1 lb. bacon, crisply cooked
  and crumbled
4 15-oz. cans tomato sauce

3 16-oz. cans kidney
  beans, drained and
  rinsed
2 T. chili seasoning
15-1/4 oz. can corn, drained

Place beef, sausage and bacon in a greased 6-quart slow cooker; stir in tomato sauce, beans and seasoning. Cover and cook on low setting for 4 to 6 hours; add corn during last hour. Serves 6 to 8.

Beef & Butternut Stew

Vickie

2 t. dried thyme
2 t. salt
3/4 t. pepper
5 T. cornstarch
1-1/2 lb. beef round roast, cubed
1 bulb fennel, sliced
3/4 lb. redskin potatoes, quartered
28-oz. can whole tomatoes, drained and tomatoes halved
1 butternut squash, peeled, seeded and cubed
1 t. olive oil

Combine seasonings in a bowl; reserve one teaspoon seasoning mixture. Combine cornstarch with remaining seasoning mixture. Toss beef, fennel and potatoes in cornstarch mixture until well coated. Transfer beef mixture to a slow cooker; spoon tomatoes over top. In a separate bowl, toss squash with oil and reserved spice mixture. Layer squash on top of tomatoes. Cover and cook on low setting for 8 hours. Serves 8 to 10.

Beef & Butternut Stew

Cream of Cauliflower Soup♪

Paula Marchesi, Lenhartsville, PA

1 head cauliflower, chopped
2 c. chicken broth
2 T. reduced-sodium chicken bouillon granules
2 c. half-and-half
2 c. milk
1 carrot, peeled and shredded
2 bay leaves
1/4 t. garlic powder
1/2 c. instant mashed potato flakes
1 c. shredded Monterey Jack cheese
1 c. shredded Cheddar cheese
Garnish: paprika or minced fresh parsley

In a large saucepan, combine cauliflower, broth and bouillon. Bring to a boil. Reduce heat, cover and cook for 20 minutes, or until cauliflower is tender. Mash cauliflower in saucepan. Transfer entire contents of saucepan to a 3-quart slow cooker. Stir in half-and-half, milk, carrot, bay leaves and garlic powder. Cover and cook on low setting for 3 hours. Stir in potato flakes; cook 30 minutes longer, or until thickened. Discard bay leaves. Cool slightly. Using an immersion blender, process soup until smooth. Stir in cheeses. Cover and cook until soup is heated through and cheese is melted. Garnish servings with paprika or parsley. Serves 8.

Quick tip

When cutting meat or vegetables, be sure the pieces are the same size so they cook evenly.

Cream of Cauliflower Soup

Papa's Favorite Cheesy Corn Soup

Papas Favorite Cheesy Corn Soup

Kristina Hodgdon, Marco Island, FL

1 c. green pepper, chopped
1 c. onion, chopped
6 cloves garlic, minced
1/4 c. butter
2 8-oz. pkgs. cream cheese, cubed
2 c. milk
2 cubes chicken bouillon
2 c. boiling water
2 8-oz. cans corn, drained
2 8-oz. cans creamed corn
6 baking potatoes, peeled and cubed
1 t. salt
pepper to taste
Optional: 1 lb. white fish, such as haddock or tilapia, or other seafood such as clams, crab, shrimp or scallops
Garnish: oyster crackers

In a skillet, sauté green pepper, onion and garlic in butter. Add cream cheese and milk. Cook and stir until cream cheese melts. Add to a slow cooker. Dissolve bouillon in boiling water. Stir into slow cooker. Add remaining ingredients except seafood, if using, and garnish. Cover and cook on high setting for 2 to 3 hours. If using, seafood may be added during the last hour of cooking time. Garnish with crackers. Serves 10 to 12.

Quick tip

You won't need much liquid; use only the amount of liquid specified in a recipe. Extra juices cook out of the ingredients, and less evaporation occurs than in traditional cooking methods.

Dan's Broccoli & Cheese Soup

Dan's Broccoli & Cheese Soup

Dan Ferren, Sheridan, IN

16-oz. pkg. frozen chopped broccoli, thawed
10-3/4 oz. cream of mushroom soup
1 c. milk
1 c. half-and-half
8-oz. pkg. cream cheese, cubed
1-1/2 c. pasteurized process cheese spread, cubed
garlic powder and pepper to taste

Combine all ingredients in a slow cooker. Cover and cook on high setting for 30 to 40 minutes. Reduce to low setting; cover and cook for an additional 3 to 4 hours, stirring occasionally. Serves 6.

Jalapeño Chicken Chili

Lisa Case, Clovis, CA

2 c. chicken, cooked and
  cubed
4 15.8-oz. cans Great
  Northern beans
2 cloves garlic, minced
1-1/2 t. ground cumin
3/4 t. salt
1/2 t. dried oregano
1 onion, chopped

1/2 c. red pepper, diced
1/2 c. green pepper, diced
2 jalapeño peppers, seeded
  and finely diced
1/2 t. chicken bouillon
  granules
1/4 c. water
1 to 2 c. salsa
tortilla chips

Combine all ingredients except salsa and chips in a slow
cooker. Cover and cook on low setting for 8 to 10 hours
or on high setting for 5 hours. Add salsa during last hour
of cooking. Before serving, stir well to blend. Serve with
tortilla chips. Serves 8.

Jalapeño Chicken Chili

Plenty o' Veggies Beef Stew

Paula Marchesi, Lenhartsville, PA

8 slices bacon, diced
3 lbs. stew beef, cubed
6 carrots, peeled and
  thickly sliced
6 tomatoes, peeled and cut
  into wedges
4 potatoes, peeled and
  cubed
3 c. butternut squash,
  peeled and cubed

1/2 c. frozen lima beans
1/2 c. corn
2 cloves garlic, minced
2 t. dried thyme
2 14-1/2 oz. cans beef
  broth
6 c. cabbage, chopped
1/2 t. celery salt
1/2 t. pepper

In a large skillet over medium heat, cook bacon until
crisp. Remove bacon to paper towels with a slotted spoon
and refrigerate; reserve pan drippings. Brown beef in
batches in reserved drippings; drain. In a 6-quart slow
cooker, combine carrots, tomatoes, potatoes, squash,
beans, corn, garlic and thyme. Top with beef. Pour broth
into slow cooker. Cover and cook on low setting for
8 hours. Stir in cabbage and seasonings. Cover; increase
to high setting and cook for 30 to 35 minutes, until
cabbage is tender. Sprinkle servings with bacon. Makes
10 to 12 servings.

Polish Sausage & Cabbage Soup

Marcia Shaffer, Conneaut Lake, PA

1-1/4 to 1-1/2 lbs. smoked
  Polish pork sausage links,
  halved lengthwise and
  sliced 1/2-inch thick
4 c. fat-free chicken broth
4 c. cabbage, chopped
2 c. potatoes, peeled and
  cubed

1 to 2 onions, chopped
1 carrot, peeled and
  shredded
2 T. caraway seed, crushed
salt and pepper to taste

Combine all ingredients in a slow cooker. Cover and cook
on low setting for 7 to 8 hours. Makes 6 to 8 servings.

Plenty o' Veggies Beef Stew

Best Beef Bourguignon

Best Beef Bourguignon p.125

Kristin Stone, Little Elm, TX

4 to 6 bacon slices, chopped
1/3 c. all-purpose flour
1 t. salt
1/2 t. pepper
2-1/2 lbs. stew beef cubes
2 to 3 potatoes, peeled and diced
1 c. onion, peeled and chopped
2 c. baby carrots
8-oz. pkg. sliced mushrooms
1 green pepper, chopped
14-1/2 oz. can diced tomatoes
2 c. beef broth
1/2 c. red wine or beef broth
1 to 2 T. garlic, minced
2 t. dried marjoram
2 t. dried basil
3 bay leaves

Cook bacon in a skillet over medium heat until crisp, about 10 minutes. Drain bacon on paper towels, reserving drippings in skillet. In a large plastic zipping bag, combine flour, salt, pepper and beef cubes; shake to coat well. Brown beef in drippings in skillet. Combine browned beef, vegetables and reserved bacon in a slow cooker. Add tomatoes with juice, broth and wine or broth; mix well. Stir in remaining ingredients. Cover and cook on low setting for 8 hours. Discard bay leaves before serving. Serves 10.

Mom's Taco Soup

Carol McClurg, Otsego, MN

1-1/2 to 2 lbs. boneless, skinless chicken breasts or tenderloins
2 to 3 c. chicken broth
24-oz. jar salsa
15-oz. can black beans
15-oz. can pinto beans
Garnish: shredded Cheddar cheese, sour cream, corn chips

Place chicken in a slow cooker; stir in broth, salsa and undrained beans. Cover and cook on low setting for 8 to 10 hours, until chicken is very tender. Shred chicken with 2 forks right in the slow cooker; stir. Serve soup with desired toppings. Serves 6 to 8.

Potato-Corn Chowder

Potato-Corn Chowder

Jerry Bostian, Oelwein, IA

2 10-3/4 oz. cans potato soup
2 14-3/4 oz. cans cream-style corn
8 slices bacon, crisply cooked and crumbled,
1 to 2 T. drippings reserved
1/2 to 1 c. milk
salt, pepper and garlic salt to taste
Garnish: fresh parsley, chopped

Blend soup and corn in a 4-quart slow cooker; add bacon along with bacon drippings, if desired. Add milk until soup is of desired consistency; add salt, pepper and garlic salt to taste. Cover and cook on low setting for 8 to 10 hours. Sprinkle individual servings with parsley. Serves 6 to 8.

Mexican Roast Pork Stew

Down-on-the-Bayou Gumbo
Sue Neely, Greenville, IL

3 T. all-purpose flour

3 T. oil

1/2 lb. smoked pork sausage, sliced 1/2-inch thick

2 c. frozen okra

14-1/2 oz. can diced tomatoes

1 onion, chopped

1 green pepper, chopped

3 cloves garlic, minced

1/4 t. cayenne pepper

3/4 lb. cooked medium shrimp, peeled

1-1/2 c. long-cooking rice, cooked

Stir together flour and oil in a small saucepan over medium heat. Cook, stirring constantly, for 5 minutes. Reduce heat and cook, stirring constantly, for about 10 minutes or until mixture turns reddish brown. Spoon mixture into a 4 to 5-quart slow cooker; stir in remaining ingredients except shrimp and rice. Cover and cook on high setting for one hour; then 5 hours on low setting. Twenty minutes before serving, add shrimp to slow cooker; mix well. Cover and cook on low setting. Ladle gumbo over cooked rice in soup bowls. Serves 6.

Mexican Roast Pork Stew
Joanne Callahan, Far Hills, NJ

4 to 6-lb. pork picnic roast, cut into bite-size pieces

1/4 c. chili powder

2 T. ground cumin

1 T. coriander

1 sweet onion, chopped

2 cloves garlic, pressed

1 T. oil

2 28-oz. cans stewed tomatoes

15-oz. can black beans, drained and rinsed

2 dried poblano peppers, finely chopped and seeds removed

2 c. apple juice or water cooked brown rice

Toss pork with seasonings. In a skillet over medium heat, sauté pork, onion and garlic in oil until browned on all sides. To a large slow cooker, add pork mixture, tomatoes with juice, beans, peppers and juice or water. Cover and cook on low setting for 9 hours. Serve ladled over rice. Serves 10 to 12.

Creamy Chicken & Macaroni Soup
Marian Forck, Chamois, MO

2 c. cooked chicken, chopped

16-oz. pkg. frozen mixed vegetables

2 c. chicken broth

10-3/4 oz. can cream of chicken soup

3/4 c. celery, chopped

2 T. dried parsley, or to taste

2 cubes chicken bouillon

20-oz. pkg. frozen macaroni & cheese dinner

Combine all ingredients except macaroni & cheese dinner in a slow cooker. Cover and cook on low setting for 4 hours. Add frozen macaroni & cheese. Cover and cook for an additional 2 hours on low setting, stirring occasionally. Makes 8 servings.

Down-on-the-Bayou Gumbo

Poblano Corn Chowder

Poblano Corn Chowder

Joshua Logan, Victoria, TX

4 c. chicken broth

1 T. sugar

2 14-1/2 oz. cans creamed corn

2 c. potato, peeled and diced

2 to 3 poblano chiles, diced and seeds removed

10-oz. pkg. frozen corn, thawed

1 lb. boneless, skinless chicken breasts or thighs, cubed

1/2 lb. chorizo pork sausage, diced

1 c. whipping cream

1/4 c. fresh cilantro, chopped

In a 6-quart slow cooker, combine all ingredients except cream and cilantro. Cover and cook on low setting for 7 to 8 hours, until chicken is cooked through. Before serving, stir in cream and cilantro; warm through. Serves 8.

Stuffed Cabbage Soup

Deborah Douma, Pensacola, FL

5 c. boiling water

4 cubes beef bouillon

1/2 head cabbage, chopped

1-1/2 lbs. ground turkey

28-oz. can crushed tomatoes

1/2 c. quick-cooking barley, cooked

1 onion, chopped

2 cloves garlic, minced

2 t. sugar

1 t. pepper

1/4 t. hot pepper sauce

Combine boiling water and bouillon cubes in a large bowl; set aside. Place cabbage in a slow cooker; set aside. Brown turkey in a large skillet over medium heat. Stir in bouillon mixture along with undrained tomatoes and remaining ingredients. Mix well and spoon over cabbage in slow cooker. Cover and cook on low setting for 8 to 9 hours. Stir before serving. Makes 8 servings.

Homestyle Ham & Bean Soup

Diane Smith, Burlington, NJ

1 lb. dried Great Northern beans, rinsed and sorted

1 meaty ham bone

2 potatoes, peeled and chopped

1 carrot, peeled and chopped

2 stalks celery, chopped

1 onion, chopped

2 t. garlic, chopped

3 14-oz. cans chicken broth

5 c. water

1 t. pepper

In a large bowl, cover dried beans with water; soak for 8 hours to overnight. Drain beans, discarding water. Add beans to a slow cooker. Add remaining ingredients; stir to combine. Cover and cook on low setting for 8 hours, or on high setting for 4 hours, or until ham falls off the bone. At serving time, cut ham off the bone; discard bone. If a thicker soup is desired, use an immersion blender to slightly mash some of the beans right in the crock. Makes 8 to 10 servings.

Quick tip

There's no need to stir ingredients unless a recipe specifically calls for it. Simply layer the ingredients in the order given in the recipe.

Hearty Carrot Soup
Kimberly Ascroft, Merritt Island, FL

32-oz. container
  sodium-free beef broth
2-1/2 lbs. carrots, peeled
  and sliced
1/4 c. onion, diced
2 cloves garlic, minced
2 T. brown sugar, packed
1 T. ground ginger
1/4 c. whipping cream

In a slow cooker, combine broth, carrots, onion and garlic. Cover and cook on high setting for 5 hours, or on low setting for 8 hours, until carrots break apart easily. Working in batches, transfer contents of slow cooker to a blender or food processor, or use an immersion blender. Blend soup for about one minute, or until desired consistency is reached. Stir in remaining ingredients. Serve warm. Serves 6.

Easy 2 x 4 Soup
Melinda Schadler, Fargo, ND

1 to 2 lbs. ground beef
1/2 c. onion, chopped
salt and pepper to taste
10-oz. can diced tomatoes
  with green chiles
10-oz. can diced tomatoes
  with green chiles and
  cilantro
2 19-oz. cans minestrone
  soup
2 15-oz. cans ranch-style
  beans or pinto beans
1-oz. pkg. ranch salad
  dressing mix
Garnish: shredded
  Cheddar cheese, light
  sour cream, crushed
  tortilla chips

In a large skillet over medium heat, brown beef with onion. Drain; season with salt and pepper. Add tomatoes with juice and remaining ingredients except garnish; simmer for about 10 minutes. Transfer mixture to a large slow cooker. Cover and cook on low setting for 2 to 3 hours, until heated through. Garnish individual servings with desired toppings. Makes 6 to 8 servings.

Loaded Potato Soup

Loaded Potato Soup
Annette Bonica, Belmont, MA

4 lbs. redskin potatoes,
  peeled and cut into
  1/4-inch thick slices
1/2 c. onion, chopped
2 14-oz. cans chicken
  broth
2 t. salt
1/2 t. pepper
2 c. half-and-half
Garnish: shredded
  Cheddar cheese, cooked
  and crumbled bacon,
  sliced green onions

Layer sliced potatoes in a lightly greased 5-quart slow cooker; top with chopped onion. Stir together chicken broth, salt and pepper; pour over potatoes and onion. Broth will not completely cover potatoes and onion. Cover and cook on low setting for 8 hours or until potatoes are tender. Mash mixture with a potato masher; stir in half- and-half. Cover and cook on high setting 20 more minutes, or until mixture is heated through. Ladle into bowls and garnish. Serves 8.

Hearty Carrot Soup

Bean & Sausage Soup

Bean & Sausage Soup

Mary Paige Boyce, Columbia, SC

48-oz. container chicken
  broth
15-oz. can black beans,
  drained
15-oz. can pinto beans
15-oz. can black-eyed peas
16-oz. smoked pork
  sausage ring, cut into
  8 sections

1 onion, chopped
1 red pepper, chopped
1 clove garlic, chopped
2 T. sugar
salt and pepper to taste
9-oz. pkg. frozen corn

In a slow cooker, combine broth, sausage, black beans and undrained pinto beans and black-eyed peas. Add remaining ingredients except corn. Cover and cook on low setting for 8 hours. Turn to high setting and stir in corn; cover and cook one hour longer. Serves 4 to 6.

Chicken & Rice Soup
with Mushrooms

Chicken & Rice Soup with Mushrooms

Linda Jancik, Lakewood, OH

1 T. olive oil
1 c. onion, chopped
1/2 c. celery, chopped
1/2 c. carrots, peeled and-
  chopped
8-oz. pkg. sliced
  mushrooms
2 cloves garlic, minced

2 c. water
5 c. chicken broth
3 c. cooked chicken,
  chopped
2 T. fresh parsley, chopped
6-oz. pkg. long-grain and
  wild rice mix

Heat oil in a large skillet over medium-high heat. Add onion, celery, carrots, mushrooms and garlic. Sauté 4 minutes, or until vegetables are tender; add water, stirring to loosen particles from bottom of skillet. Combine vegetable mixture, broth and remaining ingredients (including seasoning packet from rice mix) in a 4 or 5-quart slow cooker. Cover and cook on low setting for 4 to 4-1/2 hours, until rice is tender. Serves 8.

Chicken Enchilada Chili

Panda Spurgin, Berryville, AR

2 15-oz. cans pinto beans,
  black beans, chili beans
  or a combination
2 14-1/2 oz. cans diced
  tomatoes
2 10-oz. cans enchilada
  sauce
1 c. celery, diced
1 onion, diced

1 to 2 T. chili powder
1 t. ground cumin
4 chicken thighs and/or
  legs, skin removed
Garnish: sour cream,
  shredded Cheddar
  cheese, diced avocado,
  chopped fresh cilantro

In a slow cooker, combine undrained beans, undrained tomatoes, enchilada sauce, vegetables and seasonings. Stir gently; place chicken pieces on top. Cover and cook on low setting for 8 hours. Remove chicken to a plate and shred, discarding bones. Return chicken to slow cooker; stir. Serve garnished with desired toppings. Makes 10 servings.

Farmers' Market Stew

Verona Haught, Londonderry, NH

1/2 lb. stew beef cubes

2 1/2-inch thick boneless
   pork chops, cubed

1 T. olive oil

2 carrots, peeled and
   chopped

2 parsnips, peeled and
   chopped

2 potatoes, peeled and
   chopped

1 stalk celery, chopped

2 apples, peeled, cored and
   cut into 1-inch cubes

2 T. quick-cooking tapioca,
   uncooked

1 c. apple cider

1 c. water

2 t. beef bouillon granules

Optional: 1/2 c. red wine

1/4 t. pepper

1/4 t. dried thyme

1/4 t. dried rosemary

salt to taste

Garnish: fresh rosemary,
   fresh thyme

Brown beef and pork in oil in a large skillet over medium heat; drain. Place vegetables and apples in a slow cooker; sprinkle with tapioca. Add beef and pork. Combine remaining ingredients except salt and garnish in a small bowl; pour over beef and pork. Cover and cook on low setting for 8 to 10 hours or on high setting for 4 to 6 hours. Add salt to taste before serving. Garnish with rosemary and thyme. Serves 6.

Farmers' Market Stew

Erin's Ham & Cheese Soup

Erin Ho, Renton, WA

1 red pepper, diced

1 white onion, diced

3 to 4 cloves garlic, minced

1 jalapeño pepper,
   finely chopped and seeds
   removed

3/4 lb. cooked ham, diced

2 10-3/4 oz. cans Cheddar
   cheese soup

2 10-3/4 oz. cans cream of
   potato soup

3 c. pasteurized process
   cheese spread, diced

8-oz. pkg. shredded
   Cheddar Jack cheese

4 c. milk

1 c. whipping cream

1 t. salt, or to taste

2 t. pepper

1 T. garlic herb seasoning

Combine all ingredients in a slow cooker; mix well. Cover and cook on low setting for 4 to 6 hours, or on high setting for 2 to 3 hours, until bubbly and cheese is melted. Serves 8 to 10.

Quick tip

Fill your slow cooker at least half full but no more than two-thirds full. This helps meat products reach a safe internal temperature quickly and cook evenly.

Erin's Ham & Cheese Soup

Bacon-Corn Chowder

Bacon-Corn Chowder

Linda Keehn, Chatham, IL

5 c. redskin potatoes, cubed

16-oz. pkg. frozen corn

6 slices bacon, crisply cooked and crumbled

1/4 c. dried, minced onion

2 14-1/2 oz. cans chicken broth

1 c. water

2 t. garlic salt

1 t. pepper

1/4 t. turmeric

12-oz. can evaporated milk

8-oz. pkg. shredded Monterey Jack cheese

Optional: fresh chives, chopped

Combine all ingredients except milk, cheese and chives in a slow cooker. Cover and cook on low setting for 8 to 9 hours, until potatoes are tender. Stir in milk and cheese; cover and cook until cheese melts. Garnish with chives, if desired. Serves 4 to 6.

Turnip Greens & Pork Soup

Christy Bonner, Bankston, AL

1 lb. mild or hot ground pork sausage

1 c. onion, chopped

1-1/2 c. carrots, peeled and chopped

27-oz. can seasoned turnip greens

14-oz. can seasoned turnip greens

10-oz. can diced tomatoes with green chiles

2 15-oz. cans black-eyed peas, drained and rinsed

1 t. red pepper flakes

1/2 t. pepper

In a skillet over medium heat, brown sausage with onion and carrots. Transfer sausage mixture to a slow cooker; add greens, tomatoes with juice, peas and seasonings. Cover and cook on high setting for one to 2 hours. Serves 6 to 8.

Harvest Pork & Squash Stew

Jo Ann

1-1/2 lbs. pork shoulder roast, cubed

salt and pepper to taste

1 T. olive oil

1 onion, chopped

1-1/2 c. butternut squash, peeled and cubed

16-oz. pkg. baby carrots

8 new redskin potatoes, quartered

12-oz. jar homestyle pork gravy

1/4 c. water

1/4 c. catsup

1 t. dried sage

1/2 t. dried thyme

Season pork with salt and pepper. Heat oil in a large skillet over medium heat; add pork and onion. Cook, stirring often, until pork is browned on all sides, about 5 minutes; drain. Combine pork mixture with remaining ingredients in a large slow cooker; stir gently. Cover and cook on low setting for 7 to 8 hours. Makes 6 to 8 servings.

Turnip Greens & Pork Soup

Un-Chili

Un-Chili

Tara Horton, Delaware, OH

1 lb. ground beef
1 clove garlic, minced
14-1/2 oz. can black beans,
   drained and rinsed
1 c. beef broth
14-1/2 oz. can petite diced
   tomatoes
1/4 t. sugar
1 T. chili powder
1-1/2 t. cumin
salt and pepper to taste
1/4 to 1/2 c. water
1/4 c. frozen corn
Garnish: shredded
   Cheddar cheese, corn
   chips

In a skillet over medium heat, cook beef until almost browned. Add garlic and stir until beef is cooked through; drain. In a slow cooker, combine beef mixture, beans, broth, tomatoes with juice, sugar, seasonings and water. Cover and cook on high setting for 2 hours, or on low setting for 4 hours. Stir in corn for the last 15 minutes of cooking time. Garnish as desired. Serves 4 to 6.

Kathleen's Fabulous Chili

Weeknight Beef Stew

Karen Wilson, Defiance, OH

2 lbs. stew beef cubes
14-1/2 oz. can beef broth
11-1/2 oz. can vegetable
   cocktail juice
3 to 4 potatoes, peeled and
   cubed
2 stalks celery, chopped
2 carrots, peeled and
   chopped
1 sweet onion, chopped
3 bay leaves
1/2 t. dried thyme
1/2 t. chili powder
1 t. salt
1/4 t. pepper
2 T. cornstarch
1 T. cold water
1/2 c. frozen peas
1/2 c. frozen corn

In a large slow cooker, combine all ingredients except cornstarch, cold water, peas and corn. Cover and cook on low setting for 7 to 8 hours, until beef is tender. Discard bay leaves. In a small bowl, stir together cornstarch and cold water until smooth. Stir mixture into stew; add corn and peas. Cook on high setting for 30 minutes, or until thickened. Makes 4 to 6 servings.

Kathleen's Fabulous Chili

Kathy Murray-Strunk, Mesa, AZ

1 lb. ground beef
1/2 to 1 lb. bacon, chopped
1 onion, chopped
1 green pepper, chopped
2 16-oz. cans dark red
   kidney beans, drained
   and rinsed
16-oz. can light red
   kidney beans, drained
   and rinsed
16-oz. can pinto beans
16-oz. can pork & beans
15-1/2 oz. can Sloppy Joe
   mix
14-1/2 oz. can diced
   tomatoes, drained and
   juice reserved
1/4 to 1/2 c. brown sugar,
   packed
salt, pepper and chili
   powder to taste

Brown ground beef and bacon with onion and green pepper; drain. Combine all ingredients in a slow cooker, using half of reserved tomato juice. Cover and cook on high setting until chili begins to simmer, about one hour. Reduce to low setting; continue to simmer for 2 to 4 hours. If more liquid is needed, use remaining tomato juice. Serves 6 to 8.

Donna's Green Chile Stew

Donna Wilson, Chesapeake, VA

1 to 2-lb. boneless pork
  roast, cubed

1 onion, diced

1 T. oil

2 15-1/2 oz. cans white
  hominy, drained

28-oz. can green chile
  enchilada sauce

4-oz. can diced green
  chiles

2 to 3 cloves garlic, minced

2 potatoes, peeled and
  diced

2 carrots, peeled and
  thinly sliced

salt and pepper to taste

flour tortillas

In a skillet over medium heat, brown pork and onion
in oil. Transfer to a large slow cooker; add remaining
ingredients except tortillas. Mix well. Cover and cook on
low setting for 6 to 8 hours. To serve, scoop mixture onto
tortillas. Serves 8.

Elizabeth's White Bean Chili

Jess's Vegan Pea Soup

Jess Brunink, Whitehall, MI

2 lbs. dried split peas,
  rinsed and sorted

8 c. water

3 cloves garlic, minced

3 potatoes, peeled and
  diced

1 onion, diced

salt to taste

Combine all ingredients in a slow cooker; stir gently.
Cover and cook on low setting for 8 hours, or until peas
are tender. Makes 8 servings.

Elizabeth's White Bean Chili

Elizabeth Tipton, Knoxville, TN

1 lb. boneless, skinless
  chicken breasts, cooked
  and shredded

4 15-1/2 oz. cans Great
  Northern beans

16-oz. jar salsa

8-oz. pkg. shredded Pepper
  Jack cheese

2 t. ground cumin

1/2 c. chicken broth

Optional: 12-oz. can beer
  or 1-1/2 c. chicken broth

Combine all ingredients except optional beer or broth in
a 5-quart slow cooker. Add beer or broth for a thinner
consistency, if desired. Cover and cook on low setting for
4 hours, or until heated through. Serves 6 to 8.

Donna's Green Chile Stew

Ham & Lentil Soup

Beef Burgundy Stew ↓ P.107
Sam Littleton, Dublin, OH

6 slices bacon, chopped

2 lbs. stew beef, cubed

16-oz. pkg. frozen pearl
onions, thawed

8-oz. pkg. mushrooms,
quartered

6 redskin potatoes,
quartered

2 carrots, peeled and cut
into 1/2-inch pieces

14-oz. can beef broth

1 c. Burgundy, dry red
wine or beef broth

2 T. tomato paste

1 T. fresh thyme leaves

1 t. salt

1/4 t. pepper

3 cloves garlic, minced

2 T. cornstarch

2 t. cold water

Cook bacon in a large skillet over medium-high heat
until crisp. Remove bacon, reserving drippings in pan.
Set bacon aside. Brown beef, in batches, in drippings
until browned on all sides. Combine reserved bacon,
beef, onions and remaining ingredients except
cornstarch and water in a 5-quart slow cooker. Cover
and cook on low setting 7 hours or until beef and
vegetables are tender. Whisk together cornstarch and
water. Stir into stew. Cover and cook on high setting for
one hour or until slightly thickened. Serves 6 to 8.

Beef Burgundy Stew

Ham & Lentil Soup ↓

Megan Brooks, Antioch, TN

3 c. chicken broth

3 c. water

1 c. cooked ham, diced

1-1/2 c. celery, chopped

1-1/2 c. baby carrots, thinly
sliced

1 onion, thinly sliced

1 c. dried lentils

1-1/2 t. dried thyme

3 c. fresh baby spinach

Garnish shredded
Parmesan cheese

In a 5-quart slow cooker, combine all ingredients except
spinach and garnish. Stir well. Cover and cook on low
setting for 7 to 8 hours. Stir in spinach; let stand for a
few minutes, until wilted. Garnish each serving with a
sprinkle of cheese. Makes 6 servings.

Mom's So-Simple Chili
Nicole Wood, Ontario, Canada

1 lb. extra-lean ground
beef

1 onion, diced

salt and pepper to taste

28-oz. can crushed
tomatoes

19-oz. can kidney beans

1-1/4 oz. pkg. chili
seasoning mix

Garnish: shredded
Cheddar cheese

In a skillet over medium heat, brown beef with onion.
Drain; season with salt and pepper. Add beef mixture
to a slow cooker along with undrained tomatoes,
undrained beans and seasoning mix. Stir well. Cover
and cook on low setting for 2 to 3 hours, until heated
through. Garnish individual servings with cheese.
Makes 4 to 6 servings.

Spicy Bean & Turkey Sausage Stew ♪

Ronda Hauss, Louisville, KY

1 lb. smoked turkey sausage, halved lengthwise and sliced

16-oz. can kidney beans, drained and rinsed

15-oz. can Great Northern beans, drained and rinsed

15-oz. can black beans, drained and rinsed

1 onion, chopped

3 cloves garlic, minced

1 red pepper, chopped

1-1/2 c. frozen corn

16-oz. jar salsa

1 c. water

1 t. ground cumin

1/2 t. pepper

hot pepper sauce to taste

In a 5-quart slow cooker, combine all ingredients. Cover and cook on low setting for 6 to 8 hours. Stir before serving. Serves 6.

Zippy Sausage & Vegetable Soup ♪

Roberta Simpkins, Mentor on the Lake, OH

14-1/2 oz. can diced tomatoes

10-3/4 oz. can cream of mushroom soup

1/2 lb. smoked turkey sausage, cut into 1/2-inch slices

15-oz. can black beans, drained and rinsed

2 c. potatoes, peeled and diced

1 c. onion, chopped

1 c. red pepper, chopped

1/2 c. water

2 t. prepared horseradish

2 t. honey

1 t. dried basil

Combine all ingredients in a slow cooker; mix well. Cover and cook on low setting for 7 to 8 hours, until potatoes are tender. Makes 6 to 8 servings.

Winter Vegetable Stew ♪

Linda Belon, Winterville, OH

28-oz. can Italian peeled whole tomatoes, drained and liquid reserved

14-1/2 oz. can vegetable or chicken broth

4 redskin potatoes, cut into 1/2-inch cubes

2 c. celery, cut into 1/2-inch pieces

1-1/2 c. carrots, peeled and cut into 1/2-inch pieces

1 c. parsnips, peeled and cut into 1/2-inch pieces

2 leeks, cut into 1/2-inch pieces

1/2 t. salt

1/2 t. dried thyme

1/2 t. dried rosemary

3 T. cornstarch

3 T. cold water

Coarsely chop tomatoes and add to a 5-quart slow cooker along with reserved liquid. Add remaining ingredients except cornstarch and cold water. Cover and cook on low setting for 8 to 10 hours. About 30 minutes before serving, dissolve cornstarch in cold water; gradually stir into stew until well blended. Cover and cook on high setting about 20 minutes, stirring occasionally, until thickened. Makes 8 servings.

Quick tip

Easy clean-up! You have only one container to wash, or no container if you use heavy-duty plastic liners.

Spicy Bean & Turkey Sausage Stew

Amy's Beef Stew

Amy's Beef Stew

Amy Hauck, Portland, OR

2 to 3-lb. beef chuck roast, cubed

2 turnips, peeled and cubed

2 rutabagas, peeled and cubed

1 Yukon Gold potato, peeled and cubed

1 onion, cut into wedges

2 10-3/4 oz. cans of cream of mushroom soup

1.35-oz. pkg. onion soup mix

Place beef and vegetables in a slow cooker; stir to mix. In a bowl, combine soup and dry soup mix. Pour over mixture in slow cooker. Cover and cook on low setting for 8 to 10 hours. Serves 4 to 6.

Chili Sans Carne

Amanda Black, Carterville, GA

2 15-oz. cans no-sodium-added black beans, drained and rinsed

15-oz. can no-sodium added kidney beans, drained and rinsed

15-oz. can corn, drained and rinsed

14-1/2 oz. can diced tomatoes

6-oz. can tomato paste

1/2 c. onion, chopped

2 cloves garlic, chopped

Garnish: thinly sliced green onions

low-sodium whole wheat crackers

Combine beans and corn in a slow cooker. Add tomatoes with juice, tomato paste, onion and garlic. Cover and cook on low setting for 8 hours. Garnish with green onions; serve with crackers. Makes 8 servings.

Slow-Cooker Beefy Taco Soup

Slow-Cooker Beefy Taco Soup

Erin McRae, Beaverton, OR

1 lb. ground beef, browned

1-1/4 oz. pkg. taco seasoning mix

15-oz. can stewed tomatoes

8-oz. can tomato sauce

15-oz. can kidney beans, drained and rinsed

Stir together all ingredients; pour into a 3- to 4-quart slow cooker. Cover and cook on low setting for 6 to 8 hours; stir occasionally. Serves 4 to 6.

Easy Potato Soup

Jeanne West, Roanoke Rapids, NC

4 to 5 potatoes, peeled and cubed
10-3/4 oz. can cream of celery soup
10-3/4 oz. can cream of chicken soup
1-1/4 c. water
4-2/3 c. milk
6.6-oz. pkg. instant potato flakes
Garnish: shredded Cheddar cheese, sliced green onions, crumbled bacon

Combine potatoes, soups and water in a slow cooker. Cover and cook on high setting until potatoes are tender, about 2 to 3 hours. Stir in milk; add potato flakes to desired consistency, stirring constantly. Cover and cook on high setting an additional 2 to 3 hours longer. Spoon into bowls to serve; top with garnishes. Serves 4 to 6.

Hearty Tomato-Beef Stew

Bethi Hendrickson, Danville, PA

1 lb. stew beef cubes
Optional: 1 T. oil
6 to 7 potatoes, peeled and diced
5 to 6 carrots, peeled and diced
2 to 3 stalks celery, diced
2 10-3/4 oz. cans tomato soup
1 T. celery seed

Spray a slow cooker with non-stick vegetable spray; set aside. If desired, brown beef in oil in a skillet over medium heat. Combine beef, potatoes, carrots and celery in slow cooker; mix well. Add soup and celery seed; mix well again. Cover and cook on low setting for 7 to 8 hours. Makes 8 to 10 servings.

Easy Potato Soup

Easy Chicken Chili

Mary Little, Franklin, TN

2 to 3 5-oz. cans chicken
3 15-oz. cans Great Northern beans
2 15-1/2 oz. cans hominy
16-oz. jar salsa
2 8-oz. pkgs. shredded Monterey Jack cheese

Combine all ingredients in a slow cooker, including liquid from cans. Cover and cook on low setting for 8 hours. Serves 8 to 10.

Easy Chicken Chili

Hearty Meatball Stew

Hearty Meatball Stew

Karen Swartz, Woodville, OH

1 lb. new potatoes, cubed
16-oz. pkg. baby carrots
1 onion, sliced
2 4-oz. cans sliced mushrooms, drained
16-oz. pkg. frozen meatballs
12-oz. jar beef gravy
14-1/2 oz. can Italian-seasoned diced tomatoes
3-1/4 c. water
pepper to taste
14-1/2 oz. can corn, drained

In a large slow cooker, layer all ingredients except corn in the order listed. Cover and cook on low setting for 8 to 10 hours. About one hour before serving, stir in corn. Serves 8.

Mom's Oxtail Soup

Bobbie Keefer, Byers, CO

2 lbs. beef oxtails
salt and pepper to taste
1 T. butter
1 T. oil
1 onion, chopped
2 cloves garlic, minced
14-1/2 oz. can beef broth
2 14-1/2 oz. cans diced tomatoes
1 head cabbage, chopped
3 carrots, peeled and diced
2 t. dried parsley
1 t. dried thyme
1 t. bay leaves, crumbled

Season oxtails with salt and pepper; set aside. Heat butter and oil in a large skillet over medium-high heat. Brown oxtails on all sides; remove to a slow cooker, reserving drippings in skillet. Add onion and garlic to reserved drippings. Cook for 5 to 10 minutes, stirring often, until caramelized. Add broth to skillet; simmer for a few minutes, stirring up any browned bits in bottom of skillet. Add skillet mixture to slow cooker along with undrained tomatoes and remaining ingredients. Cover and cook on high heat for 8 hours, or until vegetables are tender and meat pulls easily away from the bones. Discard bones before serving. Makes 8 servings.

Margaret's Lentil Soup

Lory Howard, Jackson, CA

1/4 c. oil
3 c. cooked ham or canned spiced luncheon meat, diced
1/2 lb. smoked Polish or mild pork sausage links, sliced 1/2-inch thick
2 onions, chopped
1 clove garlic, pressed, or 1 t. garlic powder
12 c. water
3/4 lb. dried lentils, rinsed and sorted
2 c. celery with leaves, chopped
1 to 2 tomatoes, cut into wedges, or 14-1/2 oz. can whole tomatoes
10-oz. pkg. frozen cut leaf spinach, partially thawed
1-1/2 t. salt
1/2 t. hot pepper sauce

Heat oil in a skillet over medium heat. Add ham or luncheon meat, sausage, onion, and garlic. Cook for 5 minutes, stirring often. Drain; add to a slow cooker. Add remaining ingredients. Cover and cook on low setting for 8 to 10 hours, until lentils are tender. This soup freezes well. Serves 6 to 8.

Quick tip

A slow cooker uses less electricity than the cooktop or oven. There's no extra heat escaping, so your kitchen stays cool.

Butternut Squash Soup

Linda Jancik, Lakewood, OH

2-1/2 lbs. butternut squash, peeled, halved, seeded and cubed

2 c. leeks, chopped

2 Granny Smith apples, peeled, cored and diced

2 14-1/2 oz. cans chicken broth

1 c. water

seasoned salt and white pepper to taste

Garnish: sour cream and freshly ground nutmeg

Combine squash, leeks, apples, broth and water in a 4-quart slow cooker. Cover and cook on high setting for 4 hours, or until squash and leeks are tender. Carefully purée the hot soup, in 3 or 4 batches, in a food processor or blender until smooth. Add seasoned salt and white pepper. Garnish with sour cream and nutmeg. Serves 8.

Russian Beef Borscht

Rita Morgan, Pueblo, CO

4 c. cabbage, thinly sliced

1-1/2 lbs. beets, peeled and grated

5 carrots, peeled and sliced

1 parsnip, peeled and sliced

1 c. onion, chopped

1 lb. stew beef, cubed

4 cloves garlic, minced

14-1/2 oz. can diced tomatoes

3 14-1/2 oz. cans beef broth

1/4 c. lemon juice

1 T. sugar

1 t. pepper

In a 6-quart slow cooker, layer ingredients in order given. Cover and cook on low setting for 7 to 9 hours, just until vegetables are tender. Stir well before serving. Serves 8 to 10.

Cider Pork Stew

Mel Chencharick, Julian, PA

2 to 2-1/2 lbs. pork shoulder roast, cubed and fat trimmed

Optional: 1 T. oil

3 potatoes, peeled and cut into 1/2-inch cubes

3 carrots, peeled and cut into 1/2-inch slices

2 onions, sliced

1/2 c. celery, coarsely chopped

2/3 c. apple, peeled, cored and coarsely chopped

2 c. apple cider or apple juice

3 T. quick-cooking tapioca, uncooked

1 t. caraway seed

1 t. salt

1/4 t. pepper

Optional: snipped fresh chives

If desired, brown pork in oil in a large skillet over medium heat. Place pork in a 5-quart slow cooker. Add vegetables and apple; set aside. In a bowl, combine remaining ingredients except optional chives. Pour over pork mixture in slow cooker. Cover and cook on low setting for 10 to 12 hours, or on high setting for 5 to 6 hours, until pork is tender. If desired, top each serving with a sprinkle of snipped chives. Makes 6 to 8 servings.

Quick tip

You don't have to stand over a hot stove or watch the clock. The slow cooker works best when it's left alone to slowly simmer food. Generally, a little extra cooking won't ruin a dish.

Butternut Squash Soup

Slow-Cooker Steak Chili

Buffalo Chicken Stew

Lori Haines, Johnson City, TN

2 to 3 lbs. boneless chicken tenders

1/2 c. butter, divided

1-1/2 c. celery, chopped and divided

1-1/2 c. onion, chopped and divided

2 t. salt

1 t. pepper

1 c. carrots, peeled and chopped

2 t. garlic powder

4 15-oz. cans navy or Great Northern beans

2 14-1/2 oz. cans petite diced tomatoes

5-oz. bottle buffalo-style hot pepper sauce

1 T. chili powder

1 T. ground cumin

8-oz. bottle blue cheese salad dressing

4-oz. container blue cheese crumbles

In a slow cooker, combine chicken, 1/4 cup butter, 1/2 cup celery, 1/2 cup onion, salt and pepper. Add enough water to cover ingredients. Cover and cook on low setting for 7 hours to overnight, until chicken is tender. Remove chicken to a plate, reserving mixture in slow cooker. Shred chicken and return to slow cooker; set aside. Melt remaining butter in a skillet over medium heat. Add carrots and remaining celery and onion; season with garlic powder. Sauté until vegetables are tender, about 5 minutes. Add sautéed vegetables to slow cooker along with undrained beans and tomatoes, hot sauce and spices. Stir; add enough water to generously cover ingredients. Cover and cook on low setting for 6 to 8 hours, or on high setting for 3 to 4 hours. Shortly before serving time, combine salad dressing and blue cheese in a bowl. Serve bowls of stew topped with a dollop of dressing mixture. Serves 10.

Slow-Cooker Steak Chili

Mignonne Gardner, Pleasant Grove, UT

2 lbs. beef round steak, cut into 1-inch cubes

1-1/2 c. onion, chopped

2 cloves garlic, minced

2 T. oil

1-1/3 c. water, divided

2 15-oz. cans kidney beans, drained and rinsed

2 14-1/2 oz. cans diced tomatoes

16-oz. jar salsa

15-oz. can tomato sauce

1 c. celery, chopped

1-1/2 T. chili powder

1 t. ground cumin

1 t. dried oregano

1/2 t. pepper

2 T. all-purpose flour

2 T. cornmeal

Garnish: shredded Cheddar cheese, sour cream, crushed tortilla chips

Brown beef, onion and garlic in oil in a large skillet over medium heat; drain. Add beef mixture to a 5-quart slow cooker. Stir in one cup water and remaining ingredients except flour, cornmeal and garnish; mix well. Cover and cook on low setting for 8 hours. Combine flour, cornmeal and remaining 1/3 cup water in a small bowl, whisking until smooth. Add mixture to simmering chili right before serving; stir 2 minutes, or until thickened. Garnish as desired. Serves 8.

Quick tip

Tough, less-expensive cuts of meat transform into tender, moist and richly flavored dishes when cooked in the slow cooker.

New England Clam Chowder !

Virginia Watson, Scranton, PA

1/2 c. butter, melted

2 T. onion powder

2 t. dried thyme

2 stalks celery, chopped

46-oz. can clam juice

2 cubes chicken bouillon

2 bay leaves

3 16-oz. cans whole potatoes, drained and diced

3 10-oz. cans whole baby clams

2 c. light cream

2 c. milk

salt and pepper to taste

Stir together butter, onion powder, thyme and celery in a slow cooker; cover and cook on high setting for 30 minutes. Add clam juice, bouillon, bay leaves and potatoes. Cover and continue cooking on high setting for 2 hours. Add clams; reduce heat to low setting. Cover and cook for 2 more hours. Stir in cream and milk; cover and cook one more hour, or until heated through. Before serving, discard bay leaves; add salt and pepper to taste. Serves 6.

Spicy Chicken & Green Chile Soup

Darcy Geiger, Columbia City, IN

3 c. cooked chicken, diced or shredded

2 15-oz. cans whole tomatoes

2 15-oz. cans ranch-style beans

32-oz. container chicken broth

16-oz. jar green salsa

4-oz. can diced green chiles

2 15-oz. cans garbanzo beans, drained

Garnish: crumbled queso fresco cheese or shredded white Cheddar cheese, sour cream, crushed tortilla chips

In a large slow cooker, combine chicken, tomatoes with juice and remaining ingredients except garnish. Cover and cook on low setting for 6 to 8 hours. Stir. Garnish servings with cheese, a dollop of sour cream and some crushed tortilla chips. Makes 4 to 6 servings.

Lightened-Up Cheeseburger Soup

Marsha Baker, Pioneer, OH

P.95

1 T. olive oil

1 onion, chopped

1 stalk celery, chopped

1 clove garlic, minced

1 lb. lean ground beef

3 T. all-purpose flour

3 c. fat-free chicken broth, divided

15-oz. can fire-roasted diced tomatoes, partially drained

1 c. low-fat evaporated milk

8-oz. pkg. reduced-fat pasteurized process cheese, cubed

1/2 t. paprika

Optional: 1/4 t. salt, 1/4 t. pepper

Garnish: baked tortilla chips, crushed

Add oil to a Dutch oven; heat over medium-high heat for 30 seconds. Add onion, celery and garlic. Cook, stirring often, until tender, 5 to 10 minutes. Coat a 4-quart slow cooker with non-stick vegetable spray; spoon in onion mixture and set aside. In the same skillet, brown beef over medium-high heat, breaking up beef as it cooks. Drain and add beef to slow cooker. In a small cup, combine flour and 1/2 cup broth; stir until smooth and lump-free. Pour flour mixture into same skillet; add remaining broth. Bring to a simmer, scraping up any browned bits in bottom of skillet; pour into slow cooker. Stir in remaining ingredients except tortilla chips. Cover and cook on low setting for 2 hours. Serve soup topped with crushed chips. Serves 8.

Quick tip

Prepare hot drinks and appetizers in the slow cooker and place the cooker where your guests will gather. Just make sure to use the low setting.

New England Clam Chowder

Slow-Cooker Country Chicken & Dumplings

Slow-Cooker Country Chicken & Dumplings

Joanne Curran, Arlington, MA

4 boneless, skinless
  chicken breasts
2 10-3/4 oz. cans cream of
  chicken soup
2 T. butter, sliced

1 onion, finely diced
2 7-1/2 oz. tubes
  refrigerated biscuits, torn

Place chicken, soup, butter and onion in a 4-quart slow cooker; add enough water to cover chicken. Cover and cook on high setting for 4 hours. Add biscuits to slow cooker; gently push biscuits into cooking liquid. Cover and continue cooking for about 1-1/2 hours, until biscuits are done in the center. Serves 6.

French Lentil Soup

Marcia Shaffer, Conneaut Lake, PA

6 T. oil
1 onion, chopped
2 cloves garlic, minced
12 c. water
1-1/2 c. dried lentils, rinsed
  and sorted
1 potato, peeled and diced
1 stalk celery, finely
  chopped
1 turnip, peeled and diced

1 carrot, peeled and finely
  chopped
1 c. tomato sauce
salt and pepper to taste
1 bay leaf
1 bunch fresh sorrel or
  spinach, torn
1/2 c. cooked rice

Heat oil in a skillet over medium heat. Add onion and cook until soft, about 5 minutes. Add garlic; cook 3 minutes. Add onion mixture and remaining ingredients except sorrel or spinach and rice to a slow cooker. Cover and cook on low setting for 8 hours. Discard bay leaf. Shortly before serving time, add sorrel or spinach and cooked rice to slow cooker. Cover and cook for several minutes, until greens wilt; stir well.
Makes 6 to 8 servings.

Vegetarian Quinoa Chili

Marie Matter, Dallas, TX

2 14-1/2 oz. cans diced
  tomatoes with green
  chiles
15-oz. can tomato sauce
15-oz. can kidney beans,
  drained and rinsed
15-oz. can black beans,
  drained and rinsed
1-1/2 c. vegetable broth
1 c. frozen corn
1 c. quinoa, uncooked and
  rinsed
1 onion, diced

3 cloves garlic, minced
2 T. chili powder
2 t. ground cumin
1-1/2 t. smoked paprika
1-1/2 t. sugar
1/4 t. cayenne pepper
1/2 t. ground coriander
1/2 t. kosher salt
1/4 t. pepper
Garnish: shredded
  Cheddar cheese, sour
  cream, sliced avocado,
  chopped fresh cilantro

Combine undrained tomatoes and remaining ingredients except garnish in a slow cooker; stir together. Cover and cook on low setting for 6 to 8 hours, or on high setting for 3 to 4 hours. To serve, ladle into soup bowls; garnish as desired. Makes 6 servings.

Quick tip

The tougher cuts of meat are also the leanest, and seldom do you add fat when cooking meat and poultry in the slow cooker. During the long simmering time, fat will rise to the top of the cooking liquid; remove it before serving.

Slow-Cooker Chile Verde Soup

Lisa Sett, Thousand Oaks, CA

1/2 lb. pork tenderloin, cut into 1/2-inch cubes

1 t. oil

2 c. chicken broth

2 15-oz. cans white beans, drained and rinsed

2 4-oz. cans diced green chiles

1/4 t. ground cumin

1/4 t. dried oregano

salt and pepper to taste

Optional: chopped fresh cilantro

Cook pork in oil in a skillet over medium heat for one to 2 minutes or until browned. Place pork in a 4-quart slow cooker. Add remaining ingredients except cilantro; stir well. Cover and cook on low setting for 4 to 6 hours. Sprinkle cilantro over each serving, if desired. Serves 6 to 8.

Mom's Firehouse Chili

Wendy Lee Paffenroth, Pine Island, NY

1-1/2 lbs. boneless beef chuck roast, cubed

3 onions, sliced

2 c. water

28-oz. can crushed tomatoes

6-oz. can tomato paste

2 stalks celery, sliced

1 green pepper, cut into strips

16-oz. can kidney beans, drained and rinsed

16-oz. can white beans, drained and rinsed

pepper, garlic powder, dried parsley, chili powder and hot pepper sauce to taste

14-3/4 oz. can corn, drained

Place beef, onions and water in a 5-quart slow cooker. Add tomatoes and tomato paste; stir well. Add celery, green pepper and beans. Stir in seasonings to taste; top with corn. Cover and cook on low setting for 8 to 10 hours or on high setting for 5 to 6 hours, stirring occasionally. Serves 6.

Garden-Style Navy Bean Soup

Penny Sherman, Ava, MO

1 lb. dried navy beans, rinsed and sorted

6 c. water

14-1/2 oz. can diced tomatoes with spicy red pepper

2 c. cooked ham, diced

1 onion, chopped

3 stalks celery, thinly sliced

3 carrots, peeled and thinly sliced

1/2 t. dried thyme

1 t. salt

1/4 t. pepper

5-oz. pkg. baby spinach

In a large bowl, cover dried beans with water; soak for 8 hours to overnight. Drain beans, discarding water. Add beans to a slow cooker. Stir in 6 cups fresh water, tomatoes with juice and remaining ingredients except salt, pepper and spinach. Cover and cook on low setting for 9 to 10 hours, until beans are tender. Remove 2 cups of soup to a blender. Process until puréed; return to slow cooker. Add salt and pepper; gradually add spinach and stir until wilted. Makes 8 servings.

Quick tip

Dairy and seafood tend to break down when cooked for an extended time. Unless otherwise directed, add milk and sour cream during the last 15 minutes of cooking and put in seafood within the last hour.

Slow-Cooker Chile Verde Soup

Quick-Fix Soups

If you're short on time, these recipes will get dinner on the table lickety-split! Whether they have just a few savory ingredients or a shorter cooking time, they'll be your go-to favorites on busy weeknights. Why not give Fast Corn Chowder, Garlicky Tomato Soup or Quick & Easy Chicken Noodle Soup a try tonight?

October Bisque

October Bisque

Mary Murray, Mount Vernon, OH

1 onion, chopped
1/4 c. butter
4 c. chicken broth
28-oz. can whole tomatoes
1 T. sugar
2 15-oz. cans pumpkin
2 T. fresh parsley, chopped
2 T. fresh chives, chopped

Sauté onion in butter until onion is tender. Add broth and simmer for 15 minutes. Place tomatoes in a blender or food processor and blend until smooth. Add tomato mixture, sugar, pumpkin, parsley and chives to broth; heat through. Makes 8 servings.

Simple Beef & Tortellini Soup

Cindy Neel, Gooseberry Patch

5 c. canned beef and beans
2 14-1/2 oz. cans beef broth
2 c. frozen mixed vegetables
1 c. frozen cheese tortellini, uncooked
1 t. dried Italian seasoning
Garnish: grated Parmesan cheese

In a large stockpot, combine beef and beans, broth, vegetables, tortellini and Italian seasoning; bring to a boil. Reduce heat to medium; cook over medium heat for 8 to 10 minutes, until vegetables and tortellini are tender, stirring occasionally. Garnish with cheese. Makes 4 to 6 servings.

Quick tip

Stir some alphabet pasta into a pot of vegetable soup...you'll feel like a kid again!

Onion Soup

Penny Sherman, Ava, MO

6 onions, halved and thickly sliced
2 T. bacon drippings
6 c. beef broth
6 T. dry sherry
4 to 6 slices French bread, toasted
4 to 6 slices Provolone cheese

Sauté onions in bacon drippings. Add beef broth and sherry; simmer for 15 minutes. Ladle into individual oven-proof bowls and top each with a slice of toast. Place cheese over bread and place bowls on a baking sheet. Bake at 350 degrees for 12 to 15 minutes, until the cheese is melted. Makes 4 to 6 servings.

Chicken & Pasta Soup

John Sgambellone, Delaware, OH

2-1/2 lbs. chicken, cubed
32-oz. container chicken broth
14-oz. can chicken broth
16-oz. can green beans, drained
6-oz. can tomato paste
1 c. small shell macaroni, uncooked
1 t. dried basil

In a large stockpot, over medium-high heat, bring chicken and broth to a boil. Reduce heat, cover and simmer for 25 minutes, or until chicken is tender. Remove chicken, cool slightly. Add remaining ingredients to broth. Heat to a boil, reduce heat. Cover and simmer for 20 minutes, or until macaroni is tender. Add chicken back to soup and cook an additional 10 to 15 minutes. Makes 6 to 8 servings.

Cheesy Bacon-Wild Rice Soup ♩

Terri Peterson, New Richmond, WI

9 to 10 slices bacon, diced
1 onion, chopped
2 10-3/4 oz. cans cream of
   potato soup
1-1/2 c. cooked wild rice
2 pts. half-and-half
2 c. American cheese,
   shredded

Sauté bacon and onion together until bacon is crisp and onion is tender; drain and set aside. Combine soup and rice in a saucepan; stir in bacon mixture, half-and-half and cheese. Cook over low heat until cheese melts. Serves 6 to 8.

World's Easiest Black Bean Soup ♩

Joyce Jordan, Hurricane, WV

10-3/4 oz. can French
   onion soup
16-oz. can black beans,
   drained and rinsed
14-1/2 oz. can diced
   tomatoes with green
   chiles
1-1/4 c. water
salt and pepper to taste

Combine all ingredients in a saucepan; heat to boiling. Reduce heat; simmer for 15 minutes. Makes 6 to 8 servings.

Quick tip

Save the water that the potatoes were boiled in...add to soups and sauces to add thickness, nutrition and flavor.

Chicken Tortellini Soup ♩

Vickie

1 T. butter
3 cloves garlic, minced
3 10-1/2 oz. cans chicken
   broth
8-oz. pkg. cheese tortellini,
   uncooked
1/4 c. grated Parmesan
   cheese
salt and pepper to taste
2/3 c. frozen corn
14-1/2 oz. can Italian
   stewed tomatoes
1/2 c. tomato sauce
2 c. cooked chicken, diced

Melt butter in a saucepan over medium heat; add garlic. Sauté for 2 minutes; stir in broth and tortellini. Bring to a boil; reduce heat. Mix in Parmesan cheese, salt and pepper; simmer until tortellini is tender. Stir in corn, tomatoes, tomato sauce and chicken; simmer for 5 minutes. Serves 8 to 10.

Cream of Celery Soup ♩

Johannah Haney, Columbus, OH

1/2 c. butter, melted
4 green onions, chopped
1 bunch celery, sliced
5 potatoes, peeled and
   chopped
4 bay leaves
salt and pepper to taste
1/2 c. half-and-half

Melt butter in a large stockpot; add onions and sauté over medium-high heat, stirring occasionally. Add celery and potatoes. Add enough water to cover vegetables. Season with bay leaves, salt and pepper. Cook over medium-high heat for 30 minutes or until potatoes are tender. Remove bay leaves. Place some of the cooked vegetables, along with some of the water, into a blender. Pour in half-and-half. Blend on the highest setting until very smooth. Return mixture to saucepan and repeat until all the vegetables have been blended. Add additional salt and pepper, if needed. Makes 6 to 8 servings.

Cheesy Bacon-Wild Rice Soup

California Avocado Soup

Tomato & Spinach Soup

Joely Flegler, Tulsa, OK

2 cloves garlic, minced
2 T. olive oil
14-1/2 oz. can stewed
   tomatoes
14-1/2 oz. can diced
   tomatoes
1 to 2 c. baby spinach

In a saucepan over medium heat, sauté garlic in hot oil until tender. Stir in both undrained cans of tomatoes. Cook on medium-low heat until warmed through. Add spinach; cook and stir until spinach is slightly wilted. Serves 4 to 6.

White Bean Chicken Chili

Paulette Cunningham, Lompoc, CA

3 15.8-oz. cans Great
   Northern beans
4 boneless, skinless
   chicken breasts, cooked
   and cubed
16-oz. jar salsa
8-oz. pkg. shredded
   Monterey Jack cheese
8-oz. pkg. jalapeño cheese,
   shredded

Add all ingredients to a stockpot; cook over low heat until cheeses melt. Stir in up to one cup water for desired consistency; cook until warmed through. Serves 4 to 6.

California Avocado Soup

Charlotte Orm, Florence, AZ

1/2 c. onion, chopped
1 T. butter
2 14-1/2 oz. cans chicken
   broth
2 potatoes, peeled and
   cubed
1/2 t. salt
1/4 t. pepper
2 ripe avocados, halved
   and pitted
Garnish: 1/2 c. sour cream,
   1/4 c. real bacon bits

In a large saucepan over medium heat, sauté onion in butter until tender. Add broth, potatoes, salt and pepper; bring to a boil. Reduce heat to low. Cover and simmer for 15 to 25 minutes, until potatoes are tender. Remove from heat; cool slightly. Working in batches, scoop avocado pulp into a blender; add potato mixture with broth. Cover and process until puréed. Return to pan; heat through. Garnish with sour cream and bacon bits. Serves 6.

Quick tip

Stock your freezer with comforting home-cooked soups and stews, ready to enjoy anytime! They freeze well for up to 3 months in plastic freezer containers...just thaw overnight in the refrigerator and add a little water when reheating.

Aunties' Hot Dog Soup

Janae Mallonee, Marlboro, MA

3 potatoes, peeled and
   diced
3 onions, sliced
1 c. baby carrots, sliced
23-oz. can cream of
   mushroom soup

2-1/2 c. milk
3 to 5 hot dogs, sliced
seasoned salt and pepper
   to taste

Combine potatoes, onions and carrots in a large
saucepan; cover with water. Cook over medium-high
heat until nearly tender; drain.Whisk together soup and
milk; stir in hot dogs. Cook over medium-low heat until
warmed through. Season to taste with salt and pepper.
Makes 4 to 6 servings.

Simple Sweet Corn Soup

Karen Hibbert, Abergele, Wales

2 c. chicken broth
1/2 t. garlic powder
1/4 t. dry mustard
salt and pepper to taste
1 c. frozen corn
14-3/4 oz. can creamed
   corn

2 green onions, chopped,
   or 2 T. dried, chopped
   onion
Optional: leftover mashed
   potatoes
saltine crackers

In a large saucepan over medium heat, stir together
broth and seasonings. Add frozen corn, creamed corn
and onions; stir again. Cook for several minutes, until
corn is thawed. If a thicker soup is desired, stir in
mashed potatoes to desired consistency. Bring to a boil.
Reduce heat to medium-low; simmer for 20 minutes.
Serve with crackers. Makes 4 servings.

Cowboy Stew

Andrea Pocreva, Navarre, FL

1 lb. ground beef
salt and pepper to taste
10-oz. can diced tomatoes
   with green chiles
3 10-3/4 oz. cans
   minestrone soup

2 15-oz. cans ranch-style
   beans
15-1/4 oz. can corn
14-1/2 oz. can diced
   tomatoes

Brown ground beef in a stockpot; drain. Add salt and
pepper to taste; stir in remaining ingredients. Simmer
over medium heat for 25 minutes, or until heated
through. Serves 10.

Zucchini & Seashells Soup ↓

Judy Parks, Georgetown, TX

4 c. vegetable broth
2 carrots, peeled and
   chopped
1 onion, chopped

1 c. small shell pasta,
   uncooked
2 zucchini, grated
salt and pepper to taste

In a large saucepan, bring broth to a boil over medium
heat. Add carrots and onion; simmer for 10 minutes.
Add pasta and zucchini. Simmer for 8 to 10 minutes,
until tender. Season with salt and pepper. Makes 4 to 6
servings.

Zucchini & Seashells Soup

Texas Ranch Soup

Texas Ranch Soup

Deborah Neuman, San Felipe, TX

1-1/2 lbs. ground beef,
   browned and drained
2 15-oz. cans ranch-style
   beans
2 15-oz. cans corn
2 14-1/2 oz. cans diced
   tomatoes

1-1/4 oz. pkg. taco
   seasoning mix
Garnish: crushed
   tortilla chips, shredded
   Cheddar cheese

Combine all ingredients except garnish in a large stockpot; bring to a boil. Reduce heat and simmer for 15 minutes. Spoon into serving bowls; garnish with crushed tortilla chips and shredded Cheddar cheese. Serves 6.

Creamy Pumpkin Soup

Penny Sherman, Ava, MO

2 T. oil
1 lb. beef short ribs
4 c. water
3 c. pumpkin, peeled and
   chopped
1 baking potato, peeled
   and cubed

1 carrot, peeled and
   chopped
1 onion, chopped
salt and pepper to taste

Heat oil in a Dutch oven over medium heat. Brown ribs in oil; drain. Stir in water and bring to a boil. Reduce heat and simmer, covered, one hour. Remove short ribs from Dutch oven, cut off meat and shred; set aside. Stir remaining ingredients into Dutch oven. Simmer, covered, for 45 minutes. Pour half the soup into a blender and process until smooth. Repeat with remaining soup. Stir in reserved beef. Return to Dutch oven and heat through before serving. Serves 6.

Creamy Pumpkin Soup

Cream of Broccoli-Cheese Soup

Geneva Rogers, Gillette, WY

1 c. onion, chopped
1/2 t. garlic powder
1 T. margarine
5 c. chicken broth
8-oz. pkg. medium egg
   noodles, uncooked

10-oz. pkg. frozen,
   chopped broccoli
6 c. milk
12-oz. pkg. shredded
   Cheddar cheese

In a large stockpot, sauté onion with garlic in margarine over medium heat until onion is translucent. Add broth and bring to a boil. Reduce heat and add noodles; cook for 5 minutes. Stir in broccoli. Cover and cook for 5 additional minutes. Stir in milk and cheese. Cook slowly, stirring until cheese melts; do not boil. Makes 6 to 8 servings.

Chicken Noodle Soup for Two♩

Angie Lengacher, Montgomery, IN

2 c. water	1/8 t. pepper
2 cubes chicken bouillon	1/4 c. medium egg noodles, uncooked
5-oz. can chicken	
2 T. onion, chopped	1 T. celery, chopped
1 bay leaf	2 t. dried parsley

In a medium stockpot, bring water to a boil; add chicken bouillon and stir to dissolve. Add chicken, onion, bay leaf and pepper; bring to a boil. Cover and simmer for 8 to 10 minutes. Remove bay leaf. Add noodles, celery and parsley; simmer an additional 8 to 10 minutes, until noodles are tender. Makes 2 servings.

Creamy Potato-Ham Soup♩

Jo Ann

3 potatoes, peeled and cubed	1 to 2 c. instant mashed potato flakes
1 onion, diced	1 T. fresh parsley, chopped
1 c. water	1 t. salt
1 c. cooked ham or Canadian bacon, diced	1 t. white pepper
3 c. milk	

Simmer potatoes and onion in water in a Dutch oven until potatoes are tender. Stir in ham or Canadian bacon and milk, heating through. Add potato flakes for desired thickness; stir in parsley, salt and pepper. Serves 6.

Zesty Tomato Soup

Jane Ramicone, Berea, OH

2 10-3/4 oz. cans tomato soup	1 t. cayenne pepper
2-2/3 c. water	Garnish: oyster crackers and shredded provolone cheese
2 t. chili powder	

In a medium stockpot, combine all ingredients over medium-high heat; heat through. Spoon into individual serving bowls and garnish with crackers and cheese. Makes 4 servings.

Fast Corn Chowder

Janet Fuess, Ilion, NY

17-oz. can cream-style corn	1 t. dried minced onion
12-oz. can evaporated milk	1/8 t. pepper
12-oz. can corn with sweet peppers	1 T. butter

In a large stockpot, combine all ingredients except butter; bring to a boil. Add butter and heat until melted. Makes 4 servings.

Quick tip

If soup or stew tastes bland, just drop in a bouillon cube or two to add savory flavor in a jiffy.

Creamy Potato-Ham Soup

Navy Bean Soup

Navy Bean Soup

MaryAlice Dobbert, King George, VA

1 onion, chopped
1/2 c. butter, sliced
6 c. water
3 cubes chicken bouillon
4 c. cooked ham, shredded
1 c. instant mashed potato flakes
4 16-oz. cans navy beans
1 t. onion powder
1 t. garlic powder

In a Dutch oven over medium heat, sauté onion in butter until lightly golden. Stir in water and bouillon cubes; add ham and bring to a boil. Reduce heat to low; simmer for 15 minutes. Stir in instant potatoes; add beans with liquid and seasonings. Return to a boil, stirring constantly; reduce heat to low and simmer for 30 minutes. Makes 6 to 8 servings.

Easy Tomato Soup

Cheese Soup

Delores Hollenbeck, Omaha, NE

2 stalks celery, chopped
2 carrots, peeled and sliced
3 green onions, chopped
1/4 c. butter
2 10-1/2 oz. cans chicken broth
2 10-3/4 oz. cans cream of potato soup
8-oz. pkg. pasteurized process cheese spread, cubed
1/8 t. salt
1/4 t. pepper
8-oz. container sour cream

In a large stockpot, sauté celery, carrots and onions in butter. Add chicken broth and potato soup; cook for 30 minutes over medium heat. Blend in cheese, salt, pepper and sour cream. Simmer for an additional 15 minutes, or until cheese is melted. Makes 8 to 10 servings.

Easy Tomato Soup

Samantha Grimm, Seattle, OR

28-oz. can Italian-seasoned diced tomatoes
26-oz. can tomato soup
32-oz. container chicken broth
1/2 t. pepper
Optional: sour cream, chopped fresh basil

Pulse tomatoes with juice in a food processor or blender 3 to 4 times, or until finely diced. Stir together tomatoes, soup, chicken broth and pepper in a Dutch oven. Cook over medium heat, stirring occasionally, for 10 minutes, or until thoroughly heated. Top servings with sour cream and chopped fresh basil, if desired. Makes 8 servings.

Erma Lee's Chicken Soup

Shirley White Gatesville, TX

3 14-1/2 oz. cans chicken
 broth
2/3 c. onion, diced
2/3 c. carrot, peeled and
 diced
1/3 c. celery, diced
2 10-3/4 oz. cans cream of
 mushroom soup
4 boneless, skinless
 chicken breasts, cooked
 and chopped

8-oz. pkg. pasteurized
 process cheese spread,
 cubed
1 c. shredded Cheddar
 cheese
1 c. cooked rice

Bring broth to a boil in a stockpot over medium heat.
Add vegetables; cook until tender, about 10 minutes.
Stir in remaining ingredients; simmer over low heat
until cheeses melt and soup is heated through, about 15
minutes. Serves 4 to 6.

Erma Lee's Chicken Soup

Tea Room Broccoli-Cheese Soup

Lisa Hardwick, Plainfield, IN

1/2 c. margarine
16-oz. pkg. frozen broccoli
 cuts
2 10-3/4 oz. cans cream of
 chicken soup
2 10-3/4 oz. cans cream of
 mushroom soup

4 c. milk
16-oz. pkg. pasteurized
 process cheese spread,
 cubed

In a skillet over medium heat, melt margarine. Add
broccoli; cook and stir for 5 to 10 minutes. Add broccoli
mixture to a slow cooker; stir in remaining ingredients.
Cover and cook on low setting, stirring occasionally, for
3 to 4 hours. Serves 8 to 10.

Mexican Potato Soup

Kim Scherler, Walters, OK

2 10-3/4 oz. cans potato
 soup
2 c. milk
1 c. shredded Pepper
 Jack cheese
1/4 c. pimento cheese
 spread

15-oz. can plus 7-oz. can
 corn, drained
6 slices bacon, crisply
 cooked and crumbled
1 t. onion powder
salt and pepper to taste

In a large saucepan, mix together all ingredients over
medium heat, stirring often, for 15 to 20 minutes or until
hot and cheese is melted. Makes 6 servings.

Tea Room Broccoli-Cheese Soup

Meatball Soup

Italian Bean Soup

Julia Koons, Centerville, IN

1 lb. ground pork sausage
1 onion, chopped
1 clove garlic, minced
28-oz. can diced tomatoes
15-oz. can red kidney beans, drained and rinsed
14-1/2 oz. can beef broth
15-oz. can black beans, drained and rinsed
15-oz. can navy beans, drained and rinsed
2 T. grated Parmesan cheese
1 t. dried basil

Brown together sausage, onion and garlic in a stockpot over medium heat; drain. Add remaining ingredients; cook until soup comes to a boil. Serves 4 to 6.

Smoky Sausage Soup

Lynda McCormick, Burkburnett, TX

14-1/2 oz. can Italian stewed tomatoes
14-1/2 oz. can beef broth
1-1/2 c. water
10-oz. pkg. frozen mixed vegetables
2 c. frozen diced potatoes
1/2 lb. smoked pork sausage, sliced ✓
1/2 t. pepper
Garnish: grated Parmesan cheese

Stir together stewed tomatoes, broth and water in a stockpot; bring to a boil. Stir in vegetables, potatoes, sausage and pepper. Return to a boil; reduce heat and cover. Simmer for 5 to 10 minutes. Serve sprinkled with Parmesan cheese. Serves 4.

Quick tip

The earthy, nutty flavor of wild rice is delicious in soups, salads and sides. It's actually a grass seed, not a true rice, and takes a little longer to cook. When shopping, don't confuse it with already-seasoned mixes of wild rice and long-grain or brown rice.

Meatball Soup

Amber Belt, Lafayette, IN

14-1/2 oz. can petite diced tomatoes
6-oz. can tomato paste
1 to 1-1/2 c. onion, chopped
4 14-1/2 oz. cans beef broth
2 c. water
32-oz. pkg. frozen meatballs
1-1/2 c. orzo, ditalini or other small pasta, uncooked
salt and pepper to taste
Garnish: grated Parmesan cheese

Mix together all ingredients except garnish in a large stockpot over medium heat. Bring to a boil; reduce heat to medium-low. Cook, stirring occasionally, for 20 minutes, or until pasta is tender and meatballs are warmed through. Garnish servings with Parmesan cheese. Makes 6 to 8 servings.

Quick Cabbage Soup

Yvonne Cifani, Oxford, MI

1 lb. ground beef sirloin
2 T. oil
2 16-oz. cans stewed tomatoes
10-1/2 oz. can beef broth
2 c. water
1 t. lemon juice
1 t. Worcestershire sauce
1 head cabbage, chopped
salt and pepper to taste

In a large skillet, brown beef in oil; drain. In a large stockpot, place beef, tomatoes, broth, water, lemon juice and Worcestershire sauce; bring to a boil and simmer for 30 minutes. Place cabbage in stockpot and simmer for one hour; add salt and pepper to taste. Makes 6 to 8 servings.

Cheesy Wild Rice Soup

Tanya Graham, Lawrenceville, GA

9 to 10 slices bacon, diced
1 onion, chopped
2 10-3/4 oz. cans cream of
  potato soup
1-1/2 c. wild rice, cooked
2 pts. half-and-half
2 c. American cheese,
  shredded
Optional: Biscuit Bowls

In a skillet over medium heat, sauté bacon and onion together until bacon is crisp and onion is tender. Drain and set aside. Combine soup and rice in a medium saucepan; stir in bacon mixture, half-and-half and cheese. Cook over low heat until cheese melts, stirring occasionally. Serve in Biscuit Bowls, if desired. Serves 6 to 8.

Biscuit Bowls

16.3-oz. tube refrigerated
  jumbo flaky biscuits
non-stick vegetable spray

Flatten each biscuit into a 5-inch round. Invert eight 6-ounce custard cups, several inches apart, on a lightly greased baking sheet. Spray bottoms of cups with non-stick vegetable spray; form flattened biscuits around cups. Bake at 350 degrees for 14 minutes. Cool slightly and remove biscuit bowls from cups. Return to oven and bake 7 to 10 more minutes, until golden. Makes 8.

Spinach Tortellini Soup

Pamela Bowser, Fowler, OH

16-oz. pkg. frozen cheese
  tortellini, uncooked
1 onion, chopped
2 cloves garlic, chopped
1/4 c. olive oil
28-oz. can crushed
  tomatoes
28-oz. can diced tomatoes
10-oz. pkg. frozen spinach,
  thawed and squeezed dry
48-oz. can chicken broth
1 t. dried basil
salt and pepper to taste
1/2 c. grated Romano
  cheese

Cook tortellini according to package directions; drain. Meanwhile, in a soup pot over medium heat, sauté onion and garlic in oil until transparent. Drain; add tomatoes with juice, spinach and broth. Reduce heat to low; simmer for about 20 minutes. Add cooked tortellini, seasonings and cheese. Simmer for 5 to 10 minutes, until heated through. Makes 25 to 30 servings.

Best-Ever Brocco-Flower Soup

Sandy Coffey, Cincinnati, OH

3 c. broccoli, chopped
2 c. cauliflower, chopped
4 c. chicken broth
2 c. milk, divided
2 c. cooked chicken, diced
1 t. salt
6 T. cornstarch
1 c. shredded Cheddar
  cheese

In a large saucepan over medium-high heat, cook broccoli and cauliflower in broth until tender. Do not drain. Reduce heat to low; add 1-1/2 cups milk, chicken and salt. In a small bowl, stir cornstarch into remaining milk; mix until smooth and stir into mixture in saucepan. Cover and cook over low heat, stirring frequently, until soup is hot and thickened. Stir in cheese until melted. Makes 6 servings.

Cheesy Wild Rice Soup

Cream of Peach Soup

Cream of Peach Soup

Jill Burton, Gooseberry Patch

2 lbs. peaches
1/4 c. sugar
1 c. water
1 c. whipping cream
1/2 c. white wine or apple juice
zest of 1 lemon
Garnish: chopped and sliced peach, fresh mint sprigs and chopped mint leaves

Dip peaches, one at a time, into boiling water to cover for one minute. Plunge peaches immediately into ice water to stop the cooking process; drain and slip skins off. Cut peaches into quarters. Bring sugar and water to boil in a large saucepan over medium heat. Reduce heat and add peach quarters; cover and simmer 5 minutes. Cool. Process peach mixture in batches in a food processor or blender until smooth, stopping to scrape down sides. Stir together peach mixture, whipping cream, wine or apple juice and lemon zest. Chill for 2 hours. Garnish as desired. Makes 5 servings.

French Stew

Mary Gildenpfennig, Harsens Island, MI

1 lb. bacon, chopped
1 onion, chopped
2 14-oz. cans diced tomatoes
15-1/4 oz. can peas, drained
3 T. all-purpose flour
1 c. water

In a medium stockpot, over medium-high heat, cook bacon and onion together until onion is translucent and bacon is crisp. Add tomatoes with juice and peas; bring to a boil. Mash tomatoes and peas as they boil. Reduce to simmer. Mix flour and water together; slowly add to bacon mixture and cook until thickened. Makes 4 servings.

Quick & Easy Chicken Noodle Soup

Debbie Dunham, Lumberton, TX

10 c. water
10 cubes chicken bouillon
2 10-1/2 oz. cans chicken, drained
10-3/4 oz. can cream of chicken soup
10-3/4 oz. can cream of celery soup
1-1/2 oz. pkg. onion soup mix
8-oz. pkg. wide egg noodles, uncooked

Bring water to a boil in a stockpot; add bouillon cubes and boil until dissolved. Add chicken, soups and soup mix; return to a boil. Stir in noodles; bring back to a boil. Reduce heat and simmer until noodles are tender, 8 to 12 minutes. Makes 8 to 10 servings.

Nacho Potato Soup

Nancy Swindle, Winnemucca, NV

5-1/4 oz. pkg. au gratin potato mix
11-oz. can corn, drained
10-oz. can diced tomatoes with green chiles
2 c. water
2 c. milk
2 c. American cheese, cubed

In a 3-quart saucepan, combine contents of potato mix, including cheese sauce, with corn, tomatoes and water. Mix well; bring to a boil. Reduce heat, cover and simmer for 15 to 18 minutes, until potatoes are tender. Add milk and cheese; cook and stir until cheese is melted. Serves 6 to 8.

Quick tip

Beautiful soup, so rich and green,
Waiting in a hot tureen!
-Lewis Carroll

Cheesy Chicken & Noodle Soup

Christi Perry, Denton, TX

2 to 3 c. chicken, cooked and shredded

10-3/4 oz. can Cheddar cheese soup

4 to 6 c. chicken broth

8-oz. pkg. fine egg noodles, uncooked

1 c. milk

Optional: shredded Cheddar cheese

Combine all ingredients except milk and cheese in a large stockpot; bring to a boil over medium heat. Reduce heat; simmer until noodles are soft. Stir in milk. Spoon into bowls; sprinkle with cheese, if desired. Serves 6 to 8.

Noodles & Ground Beef Soup

Sue Utley, Papillion, NE

1 lb. ground beef, browned and drained

1 qt. water

1 onion, chopped

1 stalk celery, chopped

salt and pepper to taste

2 T. beef bouillon granules

2 T. dried parsley

1 qt. tomato juice

12-oz. pkg. wide egg noodles, uncooked

In a large saucepan, crumble ground beef into water. Add onion, celery, salt and pepper. Cook over medium heat until vegetables are tender. Add bouillon and parsley. Add juice and noodles; cook for 10 minutes, or until noodles are tender. Makes 8 servings.

Quick tip

Keep tomatoes out of the fridge for fresh-from-the-garden taste.

Quick Minestrone

Diane Darr, Eureka, MO

2 14-1/2 oz. cans chicken broth

2 c. water

28-oz. can diced tomatoes

15-1/2 oz. can kidney beans, drained and rinsed

3 c. frozen vegetable blend

1 c. medium shell pasta, uncooked

Garnish: grated Parmesan cheese

Combine broth, water and vegetables in a large saucepan. Bring to a boil; add pasta. Reduce heat, cover and simmer for 20 to 25 minutes. Sprinkle servings generously with Parmesan cheese. Serves 10 to 12.

Au Gratin Potato Soup

Leona Toland, Baltimore, MD

9-oz. pkg. au gratin potato mix

10-1/2 oz. can chicken broth

3 c. water

2/3 c. carrot, peeled and diced

2/3 c. celery, diced

1 onion, diced

1/2 c. whipping cream

salt and pepper to taste

Mix the first 6 ingredients together in a saucepan; bring to a boil. Reduce heat to a simmer; cover. Simmer for 30 minutes, or until potatoes are tender; remove from heat. Stir in cream; sprinkle with salt and pepper. Serves 6 to 8.

Yellow Squash Soup

Roxanne Bixby, West Franklin, NH

1 yellow squash, sliced

1 onion, sliced

14-1/2 oz. can chicken broth

pepper to taste

1/8 c. plain yogurt

In a medium stockpot, cook squash and onion in broth for 15 minutes over medium-high heat. Add pepper and yogurt; purée in blender until smooth. Return to stockpot and heat until warm. Makes 2 servings.

Cheesy Chicken & Noodle Soup

Grandma's Pastina

Michelle McFadden-DiNicola, Highland Park, NJ

4 c. water
3 cubes chicken bouillon
2 cubes beef bouillon
3/4 c. tiny star or alphabet soup pasta, uncooked
1/2 c. fresh parsley, coarsely chopped
1/8 t. pepper
2 eggs

Cheese, garnish

Place water and bouillon cubes in a soup pot over medium heat. Stir to break up bouillon cubes once the water is simmering. Stir in pasta, parsley and pepper; boil until pasta is tender, 3 to 4 minutes. Turn heat down to lowest possible setting. In a small bowl, whisk eggs lightly with a fork; season with salt and pepper. While stirring the soup, slowly pour in eggs. Continue stirring until eggs begin to turn white. Allow eggs to cook through, about one additional minute. Serve hot. Makes 2 to 3 servings.

Garlicky Tomato Soup

Diana Chaney, Olathe, KS

3 tomatoes, cubed
2 green, red or yellow peppers, cut into bite-size pieces
10 cloves garlic, coarsely chopped and divided
1/2 c. olive oil
2 c. water
2 t. salt
pepper to taste

Combine tomatoes, peppers and half the garlic in a food processor. Pulse until tomatoes and peppers are chopped; set aside. Heat oil in a saucepan over medium heat. Add tomato mixture and cook, stirring often, about 5 minutes. Add remaining ingredients; bring to a boil. Reduce heat to low and simmer for 10 minutes. Serves 4.

Mexican 3-Bean Soup

Kathy Mathews, Byers, TX

1 lb. ground beef
1 onion, diced
2 15-1/2 oz. cans kidney beans
2 16-oz. cans pinto beans
2 15-1/2 oz. cans navy beans
15-oz. can corn
14-1/2 oz. can stewed tomatoes
14-1/2 oz. can diced tomatoes with green chiles
1-1/4 oz. pkg. taco seasoning mix
1-oz. pkg. ranch salad dressing mix

Brown beef and onion over medium heat in a Dutch oven; drain. Add remaining ingredients; simmer over low heat for one hour. Serves 8 to 10.

Zucchini Bisque

Gloria Larue-Schantz, Breiningsville, PA

2 c. zucchini, chopped
1 c. water
1/2 c. tomato juice
1 T. onion, chopped
1 cube chicken bouillon
1/8 t. dried basil
8-oz. pkg. cream cheese, cubed

In a saucepan over medium heat, combine all ingredients except cream cheese. Bring to a boil; reduce heat to low. Cover and simmer for 20 minutes, or until zucchini is tender. Pour soup into a blender; add cream cheese and blend until smooth. Return to saucepan; gently heat through. Makes 4 servings.

Grandma's Pastina

Breads, Muffins, Rolls & Biscuits

What goes best with a warm bowl of soup? A piece of freshly baked bread, of course! You'll find so many delicious ways to complement that simmering stew, like Onion French Bread, Anytime Cheesy Biscuits, Fiesta Cornbread and Sweet Bacon Monkey Bread. There are even some new ones to try, like Praline Pecan Biscuits, Orange Marmalade Bread and Peppery Biscuit Sticks.

Cinnamon Biscuits

Cinnamon Biscuits

Deanna Brasch, Waterloo, IA

2 c. all-purpose flour	1/2 t. cinnamon, divided
1 T. baking powder	1/4 c. butter
2 t. sugar, divided	1 c. milk
1 t. salt	Garnish: melted butter

Combine flour, baking powder, 1/2 teaspoon sugar, salt and 1/4 teaspoon cinnamon; cut in butter until crumbly. Stir in milk until moistened. Drop by 1/4 cupfuls onto a greased baking sheet; brush with melted butter. Set aside. Mix remaining cinnamon and sugar together; sprinkle over biscuits. Bake at 450 degrees for 10 to 12 minutes, or until golden. Makes about one dozen.

Sugar-Topped Muffins

Karen Scarbrough, Athens, GA

18-1/4 oz. pkg. white cake mix	1/2 t. nutmeg
	1/3 c. sugar
1 c. milk	1/2 t. cinnamon
2 eggs	1/4 c. butter, melted

Blend cake mix, milk, eggs and nutmeg at low speed with an electric mixer until just moistened; beat at high speed 2 minutes. Fill paper-lined muffin cups 2/3 full. Bake at 350 degrees until golden, about 15 to 18 minutes. Cool 5 minutes. Combine sugar and cinnamon on a small plate. Brush muffin tops with butter; roll in sugar and cinnamon mixture. Serve warm. Makes 2 dozen.

Mary's Sweet Corn Cake

Mary Murray, Mount Vernon, OH

1/2 c. butter, softened	3 T. yellow cornmeal
1/3 c. masa harina	2 T. whipping cream
1/4 c. water	1/4 t. baking powder
10-oz. pkg. frozen corn, thawed	1/4 t. salt
1/3 c. sugar	

Beat butter in a large bowl with an electric mixer at medium speed until creamy. Gradually beat in masa harina; beat in water and set aside. Place corn in a food processor or blender. Pulse to chop corn coarsely; stir chopped corn into butter mixture. Combine sugar and remaining ingredients in a separate bowl; stir until well blended. Stir sugar mixture into butter mixture. Pour into a lightly greased 8"x8" baking pan; cover pan with aluminum foil. Set pan into a 13"x9" baking pan; add water one-third up around smaller pan. Bake at 350 degrees for 50 minutes to one hour, until a toothpick inserted in center comes out clean. Uncover smaller pan; let stand for 15 minutes. Scoop out servings with a small scoop; serve warm. Serves 8.

✳ Quick tip

A fun new way to serve cornbread...mix up the batter, thin slightly with a little extra milk, then bake until crisp in a waffle iron.

Angel Biscuits

Lorrie Owens, Munford, TN

1 env. active dry yeast	1 t. baking soda
2 T. warm water, 110 to 115 degrees	1 t. salt
5 c. all-purpose flour	1 c. shortening
3 T. sugar	2 c. buttermilk
3 T. baking powder	Garnish: melted butter

In a cup, stir yeast into warm water until dissolved; set aside. In a large bowl, combine flour, sugar, baking powder, baking soda and salt; mix well. Add yeast mixture, shortening and buttermilk; stir well. Turn dough onto a floured surface and knead lightly. Roll out dough about 1/2-inch thick. Cut out with a 2" biscuit cutter. Place biscuits on an ungreased baking sheet; brush with melted butter. Bake at 400 degrees for 12 to 15 minutes, until lightly golden. Makes about 2-1/2 dozen.

Whole-Wheat Popovers

Lexi Grant, Huron, OH

1/2 c. all-purpose flour	2 eggs
1/2 c. whole-wheat flour	2 egg whites
1/4 t. salt	1 T. oil
1 c. milk	

Combine flours and salt in a medium bowl. Whisk together milk, eggs, egg whites and oil in a separate bowl. Whisk milk mixture into flour mixture, whisking until smooth. Place a popover pan or six 8-ounce custard cups heavily coated with non-stick vegetable spray on a baking sheet. Place in a 425-degree oven 3 minutes, or until hot. Remove baking sheet from oven and fill cups half full with batter. Bake at 425 degrees for 30 minutes. Turn oven off; remove pan from oven. Cut a small slit in top of each popover; return to oven. Let popovers stand in closed oven 3 minutes. Serve immediately. Makes 6.

Hazelnut-Raisin Cornbread

Robin Carmen, Des Moines, IA

1 c. golden raisins	2 eggs
1 c. boiling water	14-3/4 oz. can cream-style corn
2 c. all-purpose flour	1 c. hazelnuts, finely crushed
1 t. baking soda	Garnish: honey, crushed hazelnuts
1/8 t. salt	
1 c. butter	
1 c. sugar	

Place raisins in a small bowl; cover with boiling water and let stand 20 minutes. Sift together flour, baking soda and salt. Blend together butter and sugar in a separate bowl; stir in eggs and then flour mixture. Drain raisins and pat dry. Stir raisins, corn and nuts into mixture. Mix well and pour into two 8"x4" greased and floured loaf pans. Bake at 350 degrees for 50 minutes to one hour, until a toothpick inserted in center comes out clean. Turn out of pans; garnish with honey and crushed hazelnuts. Makes 2 loaves.

---

* **Quick tip** P.192

Making butter is fun for kids. Pour a pint of heavy cream into a chilled wide-mouth jar, cap the jar tightly and take turns shaking until you see butter begin to form. When it's done, uncap the jar and rinse the butter lightly with cool water. Enjoy on warm, fresh-baked bread...yum!

Angel Biscuits

Granny's Jalapeño Cornbread

Granny's Jalapeño Cornbread

Tiffany Johnson, Grant, AL

1-1/4 c. cornmeal
1/2 t. baking soda
1/2 t. salt
2/3 c. buttermilk
1/3 c. oil
2 eggs, beaten

1 c. creamed corn
1 c. shredded Cheddar cheese
1 to 2 T. jalapeño peppers, chopped

In a bowl, mix cornmeal, baking soda and salt. In a separate bowl, mix buttermilk, oil and eggs. Stir into cornmeal mixture until most lumps are dissolved; don't overmix. Stir in remaining ingredients. Pour batter into a greased 13"x9" baking pan. Bake at 375 degrees for 30 to 40 minutes. Cut into squares. Makes 15 servings.

Bishop's Bread

Kay Demaso, Revere, MA

1-1/2 c. all-purpose flour
1-1/2 t. baking powder
1/4 t. salt
6-oz. pkg. semi-sweet chocolate chips
1 c. chopped walnuts
1 c. sweetened flaked coconut

10-oz. jar maraschino cherries, drained and halved
3 eggs, beaten
1 c. sugar

In a large bowl, sift together flour, baking powder and salt. In a separate bowl, mix together chocolate chips, walnuts, coconut and cherries; add to dry ingredients. In another bowl, beat eggs together with sugar; stir into flour mixture, blending well. Spread batter evenly in a greased and floured 9"x5" loaf pan. Bake at 325 degrees for one to 1-1/2 hours. Wrap in aluminum foil and serve the next day. Makes one loaf.

Sour Cream Dill Bread

Bec Popovich, Columbus, OH

3 c. biscuit baking mix
1-1/4 c. shredded Cheddar cheese
3/4 c. milk
1/2 c. sour cream

1 egg, beaten
1 T. sugar
3/4 t. dill weed
3/4 t. dry mustard

Combine all ingredients in a mixing bowl; stir just until moistened. Pour into a well-greased 9"x5" loaf pan. Bake at 350 degrees for 45 to 50 minutes, until golden. Let cool in pan 5 minutes. Remove from pan and cool completely on a wire rack for 2 hours before slicing. Store tightly wrapped. Makes one loaf.

> ✳ *Quick tip*
>
> Sweet, little servings of butter are easy to make with a melon baller...a charming change from butter pats. Or press butter into decorative candy molds, then chill and pop out.

Grandma's Tomato Muffins

Corinne Gross, Tigard, OR

1 c. all-purpose flour
1 c. whole-wheat flour
1/4 c. grated Parmesan cheese
2 T. sugar
1 T. baking powder
1/4 t. salt
1/2 t. dried oregano
1 egg, beaten
1 c. buttermilk
1/3 c. butter, melted
1 ripe tomato, coarsely chopped

In a bowl, combine flours, cheese, sugar, baking powder, salt and oregano. Mix well. Stir in egg, buttermilk and butter just until blended. Fold in tomato. Spoon batter into 12 paper-lined muffin cups, filling 3/4 full. Bake at 400 degrees for 20 minutes. Makes one dozen.

Quick & Easy Biscuit Rolls

Kim Hartless, Forest, VA

1 c. self-rising flour
1/2 c. milk
2 T. mayonnaise

Add flour and milk to a bowl; stir well. Add mayonnaise; stir until mixed. Spoon batter into 6 greased muffin cups, filling 1/2 full. Bake at 400 degrees for 10 to 12 minutes, until golden. Recipe may be doubled for a 12-cup muffin tin. Makes 6 rolls.

Grandma's Tomato Muffins

Perfect Lemon Bread

Nichole Sullivan, Santa Fe, TX

1-1/2 c. all-purpose flour
1-1/3 c. sugar, divided
1 t. baking powder
1/2 t. salt
2 eggs
1/2 c. milk
1/2 c. oil
1-1/2 t. lemon zest
4-1/2 T. lemon juice

Mix together flour, one cup sugar, baking powder and salt in a large bowl; set aside. Beat together eggs, milk, oil and zest; add to flour mixture. Stir until well blended. Pour into a greased and floured 9"x5" loaf pan. Bake at 350 degrees for 45 to 50 minutes. Combine lemon juice and remaining sugar in a small saucepan over medium heat; cook and stir until sugar is dissolved. Using a skewer, poke holes in hot bread; drizzle hot glaze over top and cool. Makes one loaf.

Quick tip

Make a scrumptious topping for veggies using leftover bread or rolls. Sauté soft bread crumbs in olive oil or butter until golden...sprinkle with dried herbs for extra flavor.

Quick & Easy Biscuit Rolls

Mom's Zucchini Bread

Mom's Zucchini Bread

Jamie Tomkins, Lakeside, AZ

3 eggs
1 c. oil
2 c. sugar
2 c. zucchini, grated
2 t. vanilla extract
3 c. all-purpose flour
1 t. baking powder
1 t. baking soda
1 t. salt
1 t. cinnamon
1/2 c. chopped nuts

Beat eggs in a bowl. Add oil, sugar, zucchini and vanilla; blend together. In a separate bowl, mix remaining ingredients except nuts. Add to egg mixture; stir well. Fold in nuts. Divide batter between 2 greased 9"x5" loaf pans, filling 1/2 to 3/4 full. Bake at 325 degrees for one hour, or until a toothpick inserted in the center comes out clean. Turn out loaves onto a wire rack to cool. Makes 2 loaves.

Chocolate Scones

Terry Parke, Indianapolis, IN

1 c. sour cream or buttermilk
1 t. baking soda
4 c. all-purpose flour
1 c. sugar
2 t. baking powder
1/4 t. cream of tartar
1 t. salt
1 c. butter
1 c. milk chocolate chips
1 egg, beaten
1 T. vanilla extract
Garnish: additional sugar

Combine sour cream or buttermilk and baking soda in a small bowl; set aside. In a large bowl, combine flour, sugar, baking powder, cream of tartar and salt. Cut in butter with a pastry blender; stir in chocolate chips. Add egg and vanilla to sour cream mixture; stir into dry ingredients just until moistened. Turn dough out onto a floured surface; roll or pat out dough into a round about 3/4-inch thick. Cut into wedges or cut out circles with a large, round cookie cutter. Place on greased baking sheets; sprinkle with additional sugar, if desired. Bake at 350 degrees for 12 to 15 minutes, or until golden. Makes about one dozen.

Mom's Sweet Potato Biscuits

Nancy Wise, Little Rock, AR

2 c. self-rising flour
3 T. brown sugar, packed
1/4 t. cinnamon
1/8 t. allspice
3 T. shortening
1/4 c. plus 2 T. butter, divided
1 c. canned sweet potatoes, drained and mashed
6 T. milk

Combine flour, brown sugar and spices; cut in shortening and 1/4 cup butter with a fork until crumbly. Add sweet potatoes and milk, stirring just until moistened. Turn dough out onto a floured surface and knead several times. Roll out dough to 1/2-inch thickness on a floured surface; cut with a 2-inch round biscuit cutter. Place biscuits on an ungreased baking sheet. Melt remaining butter; brush over biscuits. Bake at 400 degrees for 10 to 12 minutes, or until golden. Makes about 1-1/2 dozen.

Melt-In-Your-Mouth Biscuits

Sherri Hagel, Spokane, WA

1-1/2 c. all-purpose flour
1/2 c. whole-wheat flour
4 t. baking powder
1/2 t. salt
2 T. sugar
1/4 c. chilled butter
1/4 c. shortening
2/3 c. milk
1 egg, beaten

Sift together flours, baking powder, salt and sugar; cut in butter and shortening. Add milk; stir in egg. Turn dough out onto a floured surface and knead several times. Roll out to 1/2-inch thickness. Cut with a biscuit cutter; place biscuits on ungreased baking sheets. Bake at 450 degrees for 10 to 15 minutes. Makes one to 2 dozen.

Apple-Walnut Bread ♪

Gloria Simmons, Greenville, MI

2 c. sugar	1 t. cinnamon
1 c. oil	2 t. vanilla extract
3 eggs, beaten	3 c. cooking apples, peeled,
3 c. all-purpose flour	cored and finely diced
1 t. baking soda	1 c. chopped walnuts
1 t. salt	Garnish: additional sugar

In a large bowl, beat together sugar, oil and eggs. In a separate bowl, mix flour, baking soda, salt and cinnamon; add to sugar mixture and stir well. Add vanilla; fold in apples and nuts. Divide batter evenly between 2 lightly greased and floured 9"x5" loaf pans. Sprinkle tops with sugar. Bake at 325 degrees for one hour, or until a toothpick inserted comes out clean. Makes 2 loaves.

Quick tip

Make a fabric liner for a basket of goodies... no sewing required! Cut an 18-inch square of homespun and pull away the threads at the edges to create fringes as long as you like.

Orange-Cinnamon Swirl Bread

Patty Rogers, Chicago, IL

5-1/2 c. all-purpose flour, divided	1 T. plus 1 t. orange zest, divided
2 envs. active dry yeast	3/4 c. plus 4 t. orange juice, divided
1/3 c. dry powdered milk	
1 c. sugar, divided	1 egg, beaten
1-1/2 t. salt	1 T. cinnamon
1-1/4 c. warm water	1 c. powdered sugar
1/4 c. butter, softened	

In a large mixing bowl, combine 2 cups flour, yeast, dry milk, 1/2 cup sugar and salt. Pour in warm water (110 to 115 degrees) and blend into a thin batter. Add butter, one tablespoon orange zest, 3/4 cup orange juice and egg. Add remaining flour, 1/4 cup at a time, until dough forms a ball that comes away from the sides of the bowl. Knead 8 minutes. Place dough in a greased bowl and cover tightly with plastic wrap. Let rise in a warm place (85 degrees), away from drafts, 45 minutes. Remove plastic wrap and punch dough down. Turn onto a floured surface and divide into 2 pieces. Roll each piece into a 15"x7" rectangle. In a small bowl, combine remaining sugar and cinnamon; spread each dough rectangle with cinnamon mixture. Roll up dough jelly-roll style, starting at short side, and pinch seams together. Place in 2 greased 9"x5" loaf pans, cover with wax paper and let rise in a warm place 45 minutes. Bake at 375 degrees for 10 minutes; reduce heat to 325 degrees and bake 30 more minutes. In a large bowl, blend together powdered sugar, remaining orange zest and orange juice; set aside. Remove bread from oven, turn onto a wire rack and let cool. Spread frosting evenly over the top of each loaf. Makes 2 loaves.

Apple-Walnut Bread

Grandma Bel's Honey Muffins

Grandma Bel's Honey Muffins

Dusty Allderdice, Loma, MT

2 c. all-purpose flour	1 egg, beaten
1/2 c. sugar	1 c. milk
1 T. baking powder	1/4 c. butter, melted
1/2 t. salt	1/4 c. honey

Combine flour, sugar, baking powder and salt; set aside. In a separate large bowl, whisk egg, milk, butter and honey. Stir in flour mixture just until moistened. Fill 12 greased or paper-lined muffin cups 3/4 full. Bake at 350 degrees for 15 to 18 minutes, until a toothpick comes out clean. Serve warm. Makes one dozen.

Old-Fashioned Icebox Rolls

Muriel Gundy, Morley, MI

1 env. active dry yeast	1/2 c. cold water
1/4 c. warm water	1/2 t. salt
1/2 c. boiling water	1 egg, beaten
1/3 c. shortening	3-3/4 c. all-purpose flour
1/3 c. sugar	

In a small bowl, combine yeast and warm water (110 to 115 degrees); let stand several minutes. In a large bowl, combine boiling water, shortening and sugar. Add yeast mixture, cold water, salt, egg and flour. Mix and knead until smooth. Cover and refrigerate overnight. Form into golfball-size balls and place in a greased 13"x9" baking pan. Cover; let rise in a warm place (85 degrees), away from drafts, until doubled in bulk. Bake at 400 degrees for 12 to 18 minutes, or until golden. Makes 2 dozen.

Lemon Fans

Cindy Neel, Gooseberry Patch

2 envs. active dry yeast	2 t. lemon zest
1/4 c. warm water (110 to 115 degrees)	1-1/2 t. salt
1 c. milk	4 to 4-1/2 c. all-purpose flour
2 eggs	1/4 c. butter, melted and divided
1/3 c. sugar	

In a large bowl, dissolve yeast in water. Let stand about 5 to 10 minutes, or until foamy. In a small bowl, mix together milk and eggs. Stir milk mixture, sugar, lemon zest and salt into yeast mixture. Using a heavy-duty electric mixer fitted with a paddle attachment and set on low speed, beat in flour, 1/2 cup at a time, until a dough forms. Turn dough out onto a floured surface. Knead until smooth and elastic, about 5 to 10 minutes, adding more flour to prevent sticking. Place dough in a large greased bowl, turning to coat top. Cover loosely with a damp cloth; let rise in a warm place (85 degrees), free from drafts, about one hour or until double in bulk. Divide dough in half. On a floured surface, using a floured rolling pin, roll each dough half into an 1/8-inch thick rectangle. Brush with 2 tablespoons butter. Cut each rectangle crosswise into 1-1/2-inch wide strips. Stack 6 strips on top of each other. Cut each stack crosswise into twelve, 1-1/2-inch squares. To prepare rolls, place 6 dough squares, cut-side down, in each greased muffin cup. Brush tops with remaining butter. Cover; let rise in a warm place about 20 minutes or until almost double in bulk. Bake at 400 degrees for 10 to 15 minutes, or until golden. Transfer pans to wire racks to cool slightly. Remove rolls and cool completely on wire racks. Makes 2 dozen.

Corn Fritters ♩

Bethi Hendrickson, Danville, PA

2 c. fresh or frozen corn, cooked
1 egg, beaten
1 T. baking powder
2 c. all-purpose flour
1 T. sugar
1 t. salt
shortening for frying

In a bowl, combine corn, egg and baking powder. In a separate bowl, mix remaining ingredients. Add flour mixture to corn mixture; stir until moistened. Melt shortening 1/2-inch deep in a skillet over medium-high heat. With a small cookie scoop, add batter to skillet, a few at a time. Cook about 5 minutes on each side, until golden. Drain on a paper towel-lined plate until ready to serve. Makes one dozen.

Quick tip

Keep freshly baked bread warm & toasty… simply slip a piece of aluminum foil into the bread basket, then top it with a decorative napkin or tea towel.

Jane's Sweet Bubble Bread ♩

Jo Ann

1/2 c. butter, melted
1-1/2 c. sugar
1-1/2 t. cinnamon
2 16-oz. loaves frozen bread dough, thawed
1 c. chopped nuts, divided
2 T. dark corn syrup, divided

Place melted butter in a small bowl; mix sugar and cinnamon in a separate small bowl. Form dough into walnut-size balls; roll in butter and then in cinnamon-sugar. Place half of dough balls in a greased Bundt® pan. Sprinkle with 1/4 cup nuts; drizzle with one tablespoon corn syrup. Pack remaining dough balls on top. Sprinkle with 1/4 cup nuts; drizzle with remaining corn syrup. Cover and let rise until double in bulk. Bake at 350 degrees for 25 minutes. Cool for 3 minutes; invert onto a serving plate and top with remaining nuts. Serves 10 to 12.

Boston Brown Bread ♩

Regina Vining, Warwick, RI

1 c. raisins
1 c. boiling water
1 c. all-purpose flour
1 c. whole-wheat flour
1 c. cornmeal
1/4 c. brown sugar, packed
1-1/2 t. baking soda
1 t. salt
2 c. buttermilk
1 c. molasses

Place raisins in a small bowl; cover with boiling water and let stand 15 minutes. Combine dry ingredients in a large mixing bowl; mix well and set aside. Drain raisins and pat dry; combine with buttermilk and molasses. Add buttermilk mixture to flour mixture; stir just until blended. Pour into a greased 9"x5" loaf pan; bake at 350 degrees for one hour. Makes one loaf.

Corn Fritters

Peanut Butter Bread

Peanut Butter Bread
for toasting jelly or marshmallow
Patty Flak, Erie, PA

1-3/4 c. all-purpose flour
1/2 c. sugar
2-1/2 t. baking powder
1/2 t. salt
1/2 c. creamy peanut butter
2 eggs, beaten
3/4 c. milk

In a bowl, mix together flour, sugar, baking powder and salt. Stir in peanut butter until mixture is crumbly. Add eggs and milk; stir until well combined. Turn into a well greased 9"x5" loaf pan. Bake at 350 degrees for about 45 minutes. Remove loaf from pan; cool on a wire rack. Makes one loaf.

Kathy's Bacon Popovers
Kathy Grashoff, Fort Wayne, IN

2 eggs
1 c. milk
1 T. oil
1 c. all-purpose flour
1/2 t. salt
3 slices bacon, crisply cooked and crumbled

Whisk together eggs, milk and oil. Beat in flour and salt just until smooth. Fill 12 greased and floured muffin cups 2/3 full. Sprinkle bacon evenly over batter. Bake at 400 degrees for 25 to 30 minutes, until puffed and golden. Serve warm. Makes one dozen.

Cheese Straws
Judy Borecky, Escondido, CA

2 c. all-purpose flour
2 c. shredded extra-sharp Cheddar cheese
1 t. baking powder
1/2 t. salt
6 T. ice water
1 c. butter, softened

Combine all ingredients in a food processor or heavy-duty mixer; chill. Roll out to 1/4-inch thickness; cut into 2"x1/2" strips. Arrange on ungreased baking sheets; bake at 350 degrees for 10 to 12 minutes. Serves 4.

Mini Butterscotch Drop Scones ✓
Margaret Welder, Madrid, IA

2 c. all-purpose flour
1/2 c. brown sugar, packed ✓
2 t. baking powder
1/4 t. salt
1/3 c. butter, softened
1 c. butterscotch chips *dk. choc.*
1/2 c. pecans, toasted and chopped
1 egg, beaten
2/3 c. whipping cream
1/2 t. vanilla extract
Optional: powdered sugar

Combine flour, brown sugar, baking powder and salt in a large bowl, stirring until blended. Cut in butter with a pastry blender or fork until crumbly. Stir in chips and nuts. Combine egg, cream and vanilla in a separate bowl, whisking until well mixed. Add egg mixture to flour mixture, stirring just until moistened. Drop by rounded tablespoonfuls onto parchment paper-lined baking sheets. Bake at 375 degrees for 12 to 15 minutes, until golden. Remove from pans and cool on wire racks. Sprinkle with powdered sugar, if desired. Makes 3 dozen.

Farm-Style Cinnamon Rolls

Cindy Adams, Winona Lake, IN

16-oz. pkg. frozen bread
  dough, thawed
1/4 c. butter, melted and
  divided

1/4 c. sugar
1/4 c. brown sugar, packed
1 t. cinnamon

Place dough in a well-oiled bowl; cover and let rise to almost double its size. Roll out dough on a floured surface to a 14-inch by 10-inch rectangle. Brush with 2 tablespoons butter; sprinkle with sugars and cinnamon. Starting on one long side, roll up jelly-roll style. Pinch seam together. Cut rolled dough into 12 slices. Coat a 9"x9" baking pan with remaining butter; place dough slices in pan. Cover and let rise in a warm place 45 minutes to one hour. Uncover and bake at 375 degrees for 20 to 25 minutes, until lightly golden. Makes one dozen.

> * *Quick tip* P. 176
>
> Homemade butter on freshly baked bread... what a treat! Pour 1/2 pint of heavy cream into a small jar, close the lid tightly and shake the jar...let the kids take turns. Butter starts to form in about 5 minutes and will be ready in 10 to 15. Drain off the liquid and add a bit of salt. Yum!

Butterscotch Bubbles

Joyce Keeling, Springfield, MO

1/4 c. butter, melted
1/4 c. brown sugar, packed
1/4 c. chopped nuts

1/2 t. cinnamon
8-oz. tube refrigerated
  biscuits, quartered

Place melted butter in a shallow dish; set aside. In another shallow dish, mix together brown sugar, nuts and cinnamon. Dip biscuit pieces into butter, then into brown sugar mixture. Arrange biscuits on ungreased baking sheets. Bake at 475 degrees for 10 minutes, or until lightly golden. Serve warm. Makes about 3-1/2 dozen pieces.

Hot Chocolate Muffins

Carol Hickman, Kingsport, TN

1/2 c. butter, softened
1 c. sugar
4 eggs, separated
6 T. hot chocolate mix
1/2 c. boiling water
2/3 c. milk

3 c. all-purpose flour
2 T. baking powder
1 t. salt
2 t. vanilla extract

Blend butter and sugar together in a large bowl; add egg yolks and beat until well mixed. In a separate bowl, dissolve hot chocolate mix in boiling water; add to butter mixture along with milk. Sift together flour, baking powder and salt; add to butter mixture. In a separate bowl, beat egg whites with an electric mixer on high speed until stiff peaks form; fold egg whites and vanilla into mixture. Pour into greased muffin tins until 3/4 full. Bake at 375 degrees for 20 to 25 minutes, until centers test done with a toothpick. Makes 1-1/2 to 2 dozen.

Hot Chocolate Muffins

Swirled Coffee Cake

Last Hurrah of Summer Peach Bread

Jackie Flaherty, Saint Paul, MN

3 c. all-purpose flour	2 t. almond extract
2 c. sugar	1 t. vanilla extract
1-1/2 t. salt	3 to 4 c. peaches, peeled, pitted and chopped
1 t. baking soda	
4 eggs, beaten	Optional: 1 c. chopped nuts
1 c. oil	

Combine flour, sugar, salt and baking soda in a large bowl; mix well. Add eggs and oil; stir just until moistened. Stir in extracts, peaches and nuts, if desired. Spread into 2 greased 9"x5" or four 7"x4" loaf pans. For regular pans, bake at 350 degrees for 50 minutes to one hour. For small pans, bake for 35 minutes, or until a toothpick inserted in center comes out clean. Cool in pans for 10 to 15 minutes; remove from pans. Pour Glaze over warm loaves. Cool completely. Wrap in wax paper and then aluminum foil. Makes 2 regular or 4 small loaves.

Glaze:

2 c. powdered sugar	1 t. almond extract
2 T. milk	1/2 t. vanilla extract
1 T. butter, melted	

Mix all ingredients in a bowl to make a thin glaze.

> ✳ *Quick tip*
>
> Give breads and pastries a beautiful finish. Whisk together a tablespoon of water with an egg yolk for a golden finish, or an egg white for a shiny luster. Brush over bread just before baking...so easy!

Swirled Coffee Cake

1 drop green of green

Carol Doiron, North Berwick, ME

18-1/4 oz. pkg. yellow cake mix ✓	1 c. water
	1/2 c. oil
5-1/4 oz. pkg. instant pistachio pudding mix ✓	1/2 c. sugar
	2 t. cinnamon
4 eggs, beaten	1/2 c. chopped walnuts
1 t. vanilla extract	

Combine dry cake mix and dry pudding mix in a large bowl; blend in eggs, vanilla, water and oil. Pour half the batter into a greased Bundt® pan; set aside. Mix together sugar, cinnamon and walnuts in a small bowl; sprinkle half over batter in pan. Swirl in with a knife; add remaining batter. Swirl in remaining sugar mixture. Bake at 350 degrees for 50 minutes, or until cake tests done with a toothpick. Cool in pan and remove to a serving platter. Makes 12 to 15 servings.

Garden Path Herbal Bread

Brenda Smith, Delaware, OH

1 c. all-purpose flour	1/2 c. grated Parmesan cheese
1 c. plain yogurt	
2 T. Dijon mustard	1/4 c. fresh oregano, minced
2 t. baking powder	
1/2 t. salt	1/4 c. fresh chives, minced
3 eggs, beaten	1/4 c. fresh thyme, minced

Stir together flour, yogurt, mustard, baking powder, salt and eggs in a large bowl; blend well. Add cheese and herbs; mix well. Pour batter into an 8"x4" loaf pan sprayed with non-stick vegetable spray. Bake at 400 degrees for 45 minutes. Remove loaf to wire rack to cool completely. Makes one loaf.

Anytime Cheesy Biscuits

Naomi Cooper, Delaware, OH

2 c. biscuit baking mix
2/3 c. milk
1/2 c. shredded Cheddar
  cheese
1/4 c. butter, melted
1/4 t. garlic powder

Mix together baking mix, milk and cheese until a soft dough forms; beat vigorously for 30 seconds. Drop by rounded tablespoonfuls onto an ungreased baking sheet. Bake at 450 degrees for 8 to 10 minutes, until golden. Whisk together butter and garlic powder; spread over warm biscuits. Makes about 1-1/2 dozen.

Sweet Apple Butter Muffins ♪

Donna Meyer, Pensacola, FL

1-3/4 c. all-purpose flour
1/3 c. plus 2 T. sugar,
  divided
2 t. baking powder
1/2 t. cinnamon
1/4 t. nutmeg
1/4 t. salt
1 egg, beaten
3/4 c. milk
1/4 c. oil
1 t. vanilla extract
1/3 c. apple butter
1/3 c. chopped pecans

Combine flour, 1/3 cup sugar, baking powder, spices and salt in a large bowl; set aside. In a separate bowl, blend egg, milk, oil and vanilla together; stir into flour mixture. Spoon one tablespoon batter into each of 12 paper-lined muffin cups; top with one teaspoon apple butter. Fill muffin cups 2/3 full using remaining batter; set aside. Toss pecans with remaining sugar; sprinkle evenly over muffins. Bake at 400 degrees until a toothpick inserted in the center tests clean, about 20 minutes. Makes one dozen.

Dilly Bread

Jeanine Boehm, Pittsburgh, PA

1 env. active dry yeast
1/4 c. warm water
1 c. small-curd cottage
  cheese
2 T. sugar
1 T. onion, minced
1 T. butter
2 t. dill seed
1 t. salt
1/4 t. baking soda
1 egg
2-1/2 c. all-purpose flour
Garnish: melted butter,
  salt to taste

Dissolve yeast in warm water (110 to 115 degrees) in a cup. Combine cottage cheese, sugar, onion, butter, dill seed, salt, baking soda, egg and yeast mixture in a large bowl. Add flour one cup at a time to form a stiff dough, mixing well after each addition. Cover bowl; place in a warm place and let rise one hour and 25 minutes to 1-1/2 hours, until double in bulk. Punch down and let rise 50 more minutes to one hour. Place dough in a greased 8" round baking pan; let rise another 30 to 40 minutes. Bake at 350 degrees for 40 to 45 minutes. Brush with melted butter and sprinkle with salt while still warm. Makes one loaf.

Quick tip

When baking in dark non-stick baking pans, set the oven temperature 25 degrees lower... baked goods won't overbrown.

Sweet Apple Butter Muffins

Wild Blueberry Gingerbread

Chocolate Buttermilk Biscuits ✓

Kathy Grashoff, Fort Wayne, IN

3 T. sugar, divided
1/8 t. cinnamon
2 c. all-purpose flour
1/3 c. butter
3/4 c. buttermilk
1/2 c. semi-sweet chocolate chips
1/4 c. butter, melted

Combine 2 tablespoons sugar and cinnamon; set aside. Combine flour and remaining sugar; cut in butter until mixture is crumbly. Add buttermilk and chocolate chips, stirring just until dry ingredients are moistened. Turn dough out onto a lightly floured surface; knead 3 to 4 times. Roll dough to 1/2-inch thickness; cut with a 2-1/4 inch round cookie or biscuit cutter. Arrange biscuits on a lightly greased baking sheet; sprinkle with sugar mixture. Bake at 425 degrees for 15 minutes, until golden. Brush with melted butter. Makes one dozen.

Quick tip

Savory herbed crackers make any bowl of soup even yummier! Toss together 1-1/2 cups oyster crackers, 1-1/2 tablespoons melted butter, 1/4 teaspoon dried thyme and 1/4 teaspoon garlic powder. Spread on a baking sheet. Bake at 350 degrees for about 10 minutes, until crunchy and golden.

Grandma's Irish Soda Bread ✓

Jennifer Savino, Joliet, IL

3 c. all-purpose flour
2/3 c. sugar
1 t. baking powder
1 t. baking soda
1 t. salt
1-1/2 c. raisins
2 eggs, beaten
1-3/4 c. buttermilk
2 T. butter, melted and slightly cooled

Sift dry ingredients together into a large bowl; stir in raisins and set aside. Combine eggs, buttermilk and melted butter in a separate bowl, blending well. Add egg mixture to flour mixture; stir until well blended. Pour batter into 2 greased 9"x5" loaf pans. Bake at 350 degrees for one hour. Remove loaves to wire rack to cool completely. Makes 2 loaves.

Wild Blueberry Gingerbread ✓

Gail Hageman, Albion, ME

2-1/2 c. all-purpose flour
1 c. sugar
1/2 t. ground cloves
1/2 t. cinnamon
1/2 t. ground ginger
1 t. salt
1 t. baking soda
1/2 c. molasses
2 eggs, beaten
1/2 c. oil
1 c. hot tea
1 c. fresh blueberries
Garnish: whipped cream

In a large bowl, mix together flour, sugar, spices and baking soda. Stir in molasses, eggs, oil and tea. Carefully fold in blueberries. Spoon batter into a greased and floured 13"x9" baking pan. Bake at 350 degrees for about 35 minutes, until a toothpick inserted in the center tests clean. Cool; cut into squares and top with a dollop of whipped cream. Makes 12 to 15 servings.

Chocolate-Cherry Cream Scones

Michelle Stewart, West Richland, WA

2 c. all-purpose flour
1/4 c. sugar
1 T. baking powder
1/2 t. salt
1/2 c. dried cherries, chopped
1/4 c. mini semi-sweet chocolate chips
1-1/4 c. whipping cream
Optional: additional whipping cream, coarse sugar

Combine flour, sugar, baking powder and salt in a bowl; whisk to blend well. Add cherries and chocolate chips. Pour cream into dry ingredients, continuing to stir until a soft, sticky dough is formed. Turn out onto a lightly floured surface and knead 8 to 10 times. Pat dough into a 1/2-inch to 3/4-inch-thick circle; cut into 8 wedges. Place wedges one inch apart on a parchment paper-lined baking sheet. Brush with additional cream and sprinkle generously with coarse sugar, if desired. Bake at 425 degrees for about 15 minutes, or until golden and springy to touch. Makes 8 scones.

Quick tip

If raisins become dry or sugary, or if a recipe calls for "plumped" raisins, simply place the raisins in a bowl and cover with boiling water. Soak the raisins for 15 minutes, drain and pat dry using a paper towel.

Cinnamon-Pistachio Bread

Lucile Dahlberg, Glendale, CA

18-1/2 oz. pkg. yellow cake mix
3-oz. pkg. instant pistachio pudding mix
4 eggs
1/4 c. plus 1/2 t. oil
1/8 c. water
1 c. sour cream
1/4 c. chopped nuts
3 T. sugar
1-1/2 T. cinnamon

Combine all ingredients except sugar and cinnamon in a large bowl. Mix well; set aside. Divide sugar and cinnamon between 2 greased 8"x 4-1/2" loaf pans; divide batter evenly between pans. Bake at 350 degrees for 45 minutes. Serve warm or cold. Makes 2 loaves.

Gram's Rhubarb Coffee Cake

Judy Marsh, Allentown, PA

1/2 c. butter, softened
1-1/2 c. brown sugar, packed
1 egg, beaten
2 c. all-purpose flour
1/2 t. baking soda
1/2 t. salt
1 c. buttermilk
1-1/2 t. vanilla extract
1-1/2 c. rhubarb, chopped
1/3 c. sugar
1 T. cinnamon

In a bowl, blend together butter and brown sugar; stir in egg. In a separate bowl, mix flour, baking soda and salt. Add flour mixture to butter mixture alternately with buttermilk and vanilla. Stir in rhubarb. Pour batter into a greased 9"x9" baking pan; sprinkle with sugar and cinnamon. Bake at 350 degrees for 40 minutes. Serve warm. Serves 9.

Gram's Rhubarb Coffee Cake

Pecan Pie Muffins

Cranberry-Pecan-Coconut Loaf ✓

Diana Pindell, Wooster, OH

2 c. all-purpose flour
2 t. baking powder
1 t. salt
1 c. butter, softened
1 c. sugar
3 eggs
2 t. vanilla extract
2/3 c. milk
1-1/2 c. cranberries, chopped
3/4 c. pecans, coarsely chopped
1/2 c. sweetened flaked coconut

Combine flour, baking powder and salt in a large bowl; stir and set aside. Combine butter, sugar, eggs and vanilla in a separate large bowl; mix well with an electric mixer at low speed. Add flour mixture to butter mixture alternately with milk, beginning and ending with flour mixture; mix just until blended. Fold in cranberries, pecans and coconut; spread in 4 greased 8"x4" mini loaf pans. Bake at 350 degrees for one hour and 45 to 50 minutes, until a toothpick inserted in center comes out clean. Cool completely in pans on wire racks. Makes 4 mini loaves.

Soft Bread Pretzels ✓

Lisa Cook, Amherst, WI

1 env. active dry yeast
1 T. sugar
1-1/2 c. warm water (110 to 115 degrees)
4 c. all-purpose flour
1 t. salt
1 egg, beaten
coarse salt to taste

Dissolve yeast and sugar in water in a mixing bowl; let stand 5 minutes. Blend in flour and salt. Turn dough out onto a lightly floured surface; knead until smooth. Cut dough into 10 to 12 pieces. Roll each into a long rope. Twist into pretzel shape or desired shape. Arrange pretzels on a greased baking sheet. Brush tops with egg. Sprinkle coarse salt on top. Bake at 425 degrees for about 15 minutes, or until golden. Makes 10 to 12.

Williamsburg Bread ✓

Lori Ginther, Beverly, OH

2 8-oz. tubes refrigerated crescent rolls, divided
2 8-oz. pkgs. cream cheese, softened
1-1/2 c. sugar, divided
1 egg yolk
1 t. vanilla extract
2 t. cinnamon

Arrange one tube of crescent rolls in the bottom of a 13"x9" baking pan sprayed with non-stick vegetable spray; set aside. Mix together cream cheese, one cup sugar, egg yolk and vanilla; spread over rolls. Arrange remaining tube of rolls on top. Combine cinnamon and remaining sugar; sprinkle over rolls. Bake at 350 degrees for 30 minutes. Makes 8 to 10 servings.

Pecan Pie Muffins ✓

Melynda Hoffman, Fort Wayne, IN

1 c. chopped pecans
1 c. brown sugar, packed
1/2 c. all-purpose flour
2 eggs
1/2 c. butter or coconut oil, melted and cooled slightly

Mix pecans, brown sugar and flour in a large bowl; make a well in the center and set aside. In a separate bowl, beat eggs just until foamy; stir in butter or oil. Add pecan mixture to egg mixture; stir just until moistened. Spoon batter into 9 muffin cups greased only on the bottom, filling 2/3 full. Bake at 350 degrees for 20 to 25 minutes, until golden. Promptly remove muffins from muffin tin; cool on a wire rack. Makes 9 muffins.

Anadama Bread
April Hale, Kirkwood, NY

1/2 c. cornmeal	1 env. active dry yeast
2 c. boiling water	1/2 c. warm water
2 T. shortening	(110 to 115 degrees)
1/2 c. molasses	6 c. all-purpose flour
1 t. salt	

Stir cornmeal slowly into boiling water; mix well. Add shortening, molasses and salt; set aside to cool. Dissolve yeast in warm water; let stand 5 minutes. Add yeast mixture to cornmeal mixture alternately with flour until blended. Knead until smooth and elastic and place in large greased bowl, turning to coat top. Cover and let rise in a warm place (85 degrees), free from drafts, until double in bulk. Punch down dough; turn dough out onto a floured surface and divide in half. Knead and shape into 2 loaves. Place in greased 9"x5" loaf pans; cover and let rise again until double in bulk. Bake at 375 degrees for one hour. Cool on a wire rack. Makes 2 loaves.

✳ Quick tip

A convenient place to let yeast dough rise is inside your microwave. Heat a mug of water on high for 2 minutes. Then remove the mug, place the covered bowl of dough inside and close the door.

Pull-Apart Pizza Bread ✓
Sallyann Cortese, Sewickley, PA

12-oz. tube refrigerated flaky biscuits, quartered	1/4 c. grated Parmesan cheese
1 T. olive oil	1 onion, chopped
12 slices pepperoni, quartered	1 t. Italian seasoning
1/4 c. shredded mozzarella cheese	1/4 t. garlic salt

Brush biscuits with oil; set aside. Combine remaining ingredients in a bowl; add biscuits. Toss well; arrange in a Bundt® pan lined with well-greased aluminum foil. Bake at 400 degrees for 15 minutes. Pull bread apart to serve. Makes about 2 dozen.

Country Ham Biscuits ✓
Terri Scungio, Williamsburg, VA

2 c. self-rising flour	1-1/2 c. shredded sharp Cheddar cheese
1/2 c. plus 3 T. butter, divided	3/4 c. plus 2 T. buttermilk
1 c. cooked ham, minced	

Add flour to a bowl. Cut in 1/2 cup butter with a pastry cutter or fork until mixture resembles coarse crumbs. Stir in ham and cheese. Add buttermilk; stir with fork until a moist dough forms. Drop dough by heaping teaspoonfuls onto a lightly greased baking sheet. Bake at 450 degrees for 10 to 13 minutes, until lightly golden. Melt remaining butter and brush over hot biscuits. Makes 2 to 3 dozen.

Country Ham Biscuits

Peach Cobbler Muffins

Pimento Cheese Biscuits ♪
Bruce Howard, Galena, OH

1 c. shredded sharp
  Cheddar cheese
2-1/4 c. self-rising flour
1/2 c. chilled butter, cut
  into 1/4-inch thick slices
1 c. buttermilk

4-oz. jar diced pimentos,
  drained
additional self-rising flour
2 T. butter, melted

Combine cheese and 2-1/4 cups flour in a large bowl. Sprinkle butter slices over cheese mixture; toss gently. Cut butter into flour with a pastry blender until crumbly and mixture resembles small peas. Cover and chill 10 minutes. Combine buttermilk and diced pimentos; add buttermilk mixture to flour mixture, stirring just until dry ingredients are moistened. Turn dough out onto a lightly floured surface; knead 3 or 4 times, gradually adding additional flour as needed. With floured hands, press or pat dough into a 3/4-inch thick rectangle about 9-inch by 5-inch. Sprinkle top of dough with additional flour. Fold dough over onto itself in 3 sections, starting with one short end. (Fold dough rectangle as if folding a letter-size piece of paper.) Repeat procedure 2 more times, beginning with pressing into a 3/4-inch thick dough rectangle (about 9-inch by 5-inch). Press or pat dough to 1/2-inch thickness on a lightly floured surface. Cut with a 2-inch round cutter; place side by side on a parchment paper-lined or lightly greased 15"x10" jelly-roll pan. Dough rounds should touch. Bake at 450 degrees for 13 to 15 minutes, until lightly golden. Remove from oven and brush with melted butter. Makes 2-1/2 dozen.

Blue Cheese Spread ♪
Marion Sundberg, Ramona, CA

8-oz. pkg. cream cheese,
  softened
4-oz. pkg. crumbled blue
  cheese
1/4 to 1/2 c. dry sparkling
  white wine or sparkling
  white grape juice

cracked pepper to taste
1/2 c. chopped pecans
1/4 c. fresh chives, snipped
assorted crackers

Combine cream cheese and blue cheese. Stir in wine or grape juice until desired consistency is reached. Add remaining ingredients except crackers; blend well. Serve with crackers. Serves 12.

Peach Cobbler Muffins ♪
Bonnie Allard, Santa Rosa, CA

3 c. all-purpose flour
1 c. sugar
1-1/2 T. baking soda
1/2 t. salt

3/4 c. butter, diced
1-3/4 c. milk
15-oz. can sliced peaches,
  drained and chopped

Mix flour, sugar, baking soda and salt in a large bowl. Cut in butter with a pastry blender or a fork. Add milk and peaches; stir just until moistened. Spoon batter into 18 greased muffin cups, filling 2/3 full. Spoon topping onto muffins. Bake at 400 degrees for 18 to 20 minutes, until golden. Turn out and cool slightly on a wire rack; serve warm or cooled. Makes 1-1/2 dozen.

Topping:

2 T. butter, diced
2 T. sugar

1/2 t. cinnamon

Mix together in a small bowl until crumbly.

lightly mashed S. Berries

Strawberry Scones ✓
Jennifer Wickes, Pine Beach, NJ

2 c. all-purpose flour	1 t. vanilla extract
1/3 c. sugar	1/4 c. whipping cream
2 t. baking powder	1/4 c. buttermilk
1/4 t. salt	1 c. strawberries, hulled
1/3 c. butter	and sliced
1 egg, beaten	Optional: sugar

Combine flour, sugar, baking powder and salt in a large mixing bowl; cut in butter with a pastry blender or 2 forks until crumbly. Form a well in center; set aside. Whisk together egg, vanilla, cream and buttermilk; add to dry ingredients, stirring until just moistened. Fold in strawberries; turn dough out onto a lightly floured surface and knead until smooth, about 10 seconds. Pat into a 7-inch circle about one-inch thick; slice into 8 wedges. Arrange on a parchment paper-lined baking sheet; brush with Glaze and sprinkle with additional sugar, if desired. Bake at 375 degrees for 15 minutes, or until golden. Cool on a wire rack. Makes 8.

Glaze:

1 egg, beaten	1 T. whipping cream

Whisk egg and cream together.

Quick tip

A primitive wooden dough bowl is so useful! When it isn't filled with rising bread dough, set it on the kitchen table and add shiny red apples for a quick & easy centerpiece.

Banana Nut Bread ✓
Beth Goblirsch, Minneapolis, MN

1 c. sugar	2 eggs
8-oz. pkg. cream cheese, softened	2 c. biscuit baking mix
1 c. bananas, mashed	1/2 c. chopped pecans

Blend sugar and cream cheese; beat in bananas and eggs. Add baking mix and pecans; stir until moistened. Pour into a greased 9"x5" loaf pan; bake at 350 degrees for one hour. Cool before slicing. Makes one loaf.

Cheddar-Chive Bites ✓
Jean Martin, Hingham, MA

2-1/2 c. biscuit baking mix	3 T. fresh chives, snipped and divided
1 c. shredded Cheddar cheese	2 5-oz. containers garlic & herb cheese spread, softened
3/4 c. milk	
1/8 t. garlic powder	Garnish: thinly sliced cucumber and radish
6 T. butter, melted and divided	

Combine baking mix, cheese, milk, garlic powder and 2 tablespoons butter; mix well. Drop by tablespoonfuls onto ungreased baking sheets. Bake at 400 degrees for 10 to 12 minutes, just until golden. Mix remaining butter and one tablespoon chives; brush over warm biscuits. Split biscuits; set aside. Blend cheese spread and remaining chives. Spread lightly onto bottom halves of biscuits; add cucumber, radish and top halves. Makes 2 to 3 dozen.

Cheddar-Chive Bites

Easy Stromboli

Mom's Applesauce Muffins

Emily Johnson, Pocatello, ID

1/2 c. butter, softened
1 c. sugar
1 c. applesauce
1 egg, beaten
2 c. all-purpose flour
1 t. baking soda
1 t. cinnamon
1/2 t. ground cloves
1/4 t. salt
1 c. raisins

Combine butter, sugar, applesauce and egg. In a separate bowl, combine flour, baking soda, cinnamon, cloves and salt; stir into butter mixture just until moistened. Stir in raisins. Fill paper-lined muffin cups 3/4 full; sprinkle with Crumb Topping. Bake at 350 degrees for 25 to 30 minutes. Makes 12 to 16.

Crumb Topping:

1/2 c. butter, softened
3/4 c. all-purpose flour
3/4 c. quick-cooking oats, uncooked
1/2 c. brown sugar, packed
2 t. cinnamon

Blend all ingredients until crumbly.

Easy Stromboli

Jane Evans, DeGraff, OH

1 loaf frozen bread dough, thawed
2 eggs, separated
2 T. oil
1 t. dried oregano
1 t. dried parsley
1/2 t. garlic powder
1/4 t. pepper
4-oz. pkg. sliced pepperoni
8-oz. pkg. shredded mozzarella cheese
1 T. grated Parmesan cheese

On a lightly floured surface, roll out dough into a 15-inch by 12-inch rectangle. Combine egg yolks, oil and seasonings; spread over dough. Arrange pepperoni and mozzarella cheese over dough; sprinkle with Parmesan cheese. Starting at one long side, roll up; pinch ends to seal. Place seam-side down on a lightly greased baking sheet. Brush with beaten egg whites. Bake at 350 degrees for 30 to 40 minutes, until golden. Slice; serve warm. Makes 8 servings.

Maple-Pecan Spread

Jo Ann

8-oz. pkg. cream cheese, softened
2 T. maple syrup
1/2 t. maple extract
1/2 t. cinnamon
1/2 c. chopped pecans, toasted

Beat cream cheese with syrup, extract and cinnamon until well mixed. Fold in walnuts. Let stand 20 to 30 minutes to allow flavors to blend before serving. Keep refrigerated. Makes about 1-1/2 cups.

Broccoli Cornbread

Cathy Jackson, Iona, ID

1/2 c. butter, melted
1 onion, chopped
10-oz. pkg. frozen broccoli, cooked and drained
4 eggs, beaten
1/4 c. buttermilk
8-oz. pkg. shredded Cheddar cheese
7-oz. pkg. cornbread mix

Pour melted butter into a bowl; add onion, broccoli, eggs, buttermilk and cheese. Mix well; stir in cornbread mix. Spoon into a greased 13"x9" baking pan; bake at 375 degrees for 25 to 30 minutes. Serves 12 to 14.

Quick tip

An old-fashioned bread box makes a handy storage place in the pantry for seasoning mix packets and other small items.

Blue Cheese Cut-Out Crackers ❧ *P. 219*

Sara Jackson, Thornville, OH

1 c. all-purpose flour
1/4 c. plus 3 T. butter, softened
1/4 c. plus 3 T. crumbled blue cheese
1/2 t. dried parsley
1 egg yolk
1/4 t. salt
4 t. whipping cream
1/4 t. cayenne pepper

Mix all ingredients together; let stand 30 minutes. Turn dough out onto a floured surface and roll to about 1/8-inch thickness. Use your favorite cookie cutters (flowers, teacups, wedding bells) to cut out the crackers. Place on ungreased baking sheets; bake at 400 degrees for 8 to 10 minutes, just until golden. Cool completely on baking sheets. Carefully remove the delicate crackers when cool. Makes 1-1/2 to 2 dozen.

Quick tip

Snap up stoneware butter crocks when you find them at flea markets. They're just the right size for serving party spreads and dips as well as butter.

S'mores Muffins

Brenda Huey, Geneva, IN

1 c. shortening
4 eggs
1 c. sour cream
2 c. sugar
1/4 c. baking cocoa
2 t. salt
3 c. all-purpose flour
2 t. baking soda
1 t. cinnamon
1 c. graham crackers, crushed
1 c. mini marshmallows
1 c. semi-sweet chocolate chips
Garnish: marshmallow creme, graham cracker crumbs

Combine shortening, eggs, sour cream and sugar; set aside. Mix together remaining ingredients except garnish in a separate mixing bowl; add shortening mixture to cocoa mixture and stir well. Fill greased muffin tins 3/4 full and bake at 325 degrees for 30 to 40 minutes. Cool in pan 20 minutes; remove muffins from pans. Garnish muffins with marshmallow creme and graham cracker crumbs. Makes 2 dozen.

Herbed Cheese Focaccia ♪

Mary Ann Johnson, Sycamore, IL

13.8-oz. tube refrigerated pizza dough
1 onion, finely chopped
2 cloves garlic, minced
2 T. olive oil
1 t. dried basil
1 t. dried oregano
1/2 t. dried rosemary
1 c. shredded mozzarella cheese

Unroll dough on a greased baking sheet. Press with fingers to form indentations; set aside. Sauté onion and garlic in oil in a skillet; remove from heat. stir in herbs; spread mixture evenly over dough. Sprinkle with cheese. Bake at 400 degrees for 10 to 15 minutes, until golden. Slice into squares. Makes 12 to 14 servings.

Herbed Cheese Focaccia

Spiedini

Golden Butter Rolls

Susan Ingersoll, Cleveland, OH

1 c. milk
1-1/4 c. butter, divided ✓
1 env. active dry yeast
1/2 c. plus 1 t. sugar, divided
1/2 c. warm water (110 to 115 degrees)

1 t. salt
3 eggs, beaten
1 c. whole-wheat flour
3-1/2 to 4 c. all-purpose flour

In a heavy saucepan, heat milk and 1/2 cup butter. Remove from heat and cool. In a small bowl, dissolve yeast and one teaspoon sugar in warm water. When mixture foams, add to a large mixing bowl with remaining sugar, salt, eggs and flours. Add the cooled milk mixture and blend until smooth. Turn dough out onto a lightly floured surface; knead until smooth and elastic. Place in a large greased bowl, turning to coat top; brush top of dough with 1/4 cup softened butter. Cover and let rise in a warm place (85 degrees), free from drafts, until double in bulk. Divide dough into 3 portions. Roll each portion into a 1/2-inch thick circle. Cut each circle into 10 to 12 pie-shaped wedges. Roll up each wedge beginning at wide end and place one inch apart on a greased baking sheet. Brush tops of rolls with 1/4 cup softened butter; let rise until double in bulk. Bake at 375 degrees for 15 to 20 minutes, until golden. Remove and brush with remaining butter while rolls are still warm. Makes 2-1/2 to 3 dozen.

Easy Cheesy Parmesan Bread

Denise Hazen, Cincinnati, OH

2 10-oz. tubes refrigerated biscuits
1 c. butter, melted

1 c. shredded Parmesan cheese

Dip each biscuit in butter; roll in cheese. Place in a greased and floured Bundt® pan; drizzle with remaining butter. Bake at 375 degrees for 25 to 30 minutes, or until golden. Turn out of pan while still warm. Serves 8 to 10.

Spiedini

Michelle Hill, Suwanee, GA

1 loaf French bread, sliced 1/4-inch thick
1 t. butter, softened
1/4-lb. provolone cheese, sliced 1/4-inch thick and quartered

16 4-inch sprigs fresh rosemary

Lightly spread 12 slices bread with butter on both sides. Form stacked sandwiches, alternating 3 bread slices with 2 cheese slices. Cut sandwiches into quarters with a serrated knife. Remove leaves from one end of each rosemary spring; push this end through a quartered sandwich to secure. Repeat with remaining bread, cheese and rosemary sprig. Arrange on an ungreased aluminum foil-lined baking sheet. Bake at 425 degrees for 4 to 5 minutes, until golden and cheese melts. Serve warm. Makes 16 servings.

✳ Quick tip

Use lemon juice to freshen an old wooden breadboard. Brush juice generously over the surface and let stand for 30 minutes. Then scrub with a moistened cloth and a little baking soda, rinse and let dry.

Orange-Glazed Chocolate Rolls

Geneva Rogers, Gillette, WY

3 c. all-purpose flour, divided
2 env. active dry yeast
1 t. salt
1 t. cinnamon
1-1/4 c. water
1/3 c. sugar
1/3 c. butter
1 egg
Optional: 1/2 c. raisins
1 c. semi-sweet chocolate chips

Stir together 1-1/2 cups flour, yeast, salt and cinnamon in a large bowl. Combine water, sugar and butter in a saucepan over medium-low heat, stirring constantly until butter is almost melted (115 to 120 degrees). Add sugar mixture to flour mixture; blend until smooth. Mix in egg; stir in remaining flour. Fold in raisins, if desired. Cover dough and let rise in a warm place (85 degrees), free from drafts, for one hour, until double in bulk. Punch down dough; let rest for 10 minutes. Fold in chocolate chips; fill greased muffin cups 2/3 full. Cover; let rise until double in bulk. Bake at 425 degrees for 10 to 15 minutes, until golden. Remove from pan and cool completely. Drizzle with Glaze before serving. Makes about 1-1/2 dozen.

Glaze:

1/2 c. powdered sugar
3 t. orange juice

Combine sugar and juice in a small bowl; stir until smooth and creamy.

Quick tip

Fresh-baked bread freezes beautifully. Cool and wrap it in plastic, then aluminum foil and freeze up to 3 weeks.

Melt-in-Your-Mouth Pecan Rolls ♩

Joyceann Dreibelbis, Wooster, OH

1/2 c. brown sugar, packed
1/2 c. butter, softened
1/4 c. corn syrup
2 8-oz. tubes refrigerated ✓ crescent dinner rolls
2/3 c. chopped pecans
1/4 c. sugar
1 t. cinnamon

In a small bowl, blend brown sugar, butter and corn syrup. Divide mixture between 2 greased 8"x8" baking pans; spread to coat bottoms and set aside. Unroll each tube of dough into a rectangle; press to seal perforations. Combine pecans, sugar and cinnamon; sprinkle over dough. Separately roll up each rectangle, jelly-roll style, starting on one long side; seal edges. Cut each roll into 16 slices. Place slices cut-side down in pans. Bake at 375 degrees for 13 to 16 minutes, until golden. Cool in pans for one minute; turn rolls out onto serving plates Makes about 2-1/2 dozen.

Mushroom Turnovers ♩

Judy Borecky, Escondido, CA

8-oz. pkg. cream cheese, softened
1 c. plus 2 T. margarine, divided
2 c. plus 2 T. all-purpose flour, divided
4 c. sliced mushrooms, chopped
2/3 c. green onions, chopped
1/3 c. sour cream
2 T. all-purpose flour
1/4 t. dried thyme
1/4 t. salt
1 egg white, beaten
Garnish; sesame seed

Blend cream cheese, one cup margarine and 2 cups flour; chill. In a skillet, sauté mushrooms and onions in remaining margarine for 3 minutes. Add sour cream, remaining flour, thyme and salt. Cook for several more minutes, stirring occasionally. Divided chilled dough in half; roll out 1/8-inch thick and cut with a 2-1/2" round cutter. Place heaping 1/4 teaspoon mushroom mixture in center of circle. Fold over; press edges gently with fingers to seal. Use a spatula to transfer turnovers to a lightly greased baking sheet; press edges with a fork. Brush turnovers with egg white; sprinkle with sesame seed. Bake at 350 degrees for 20 minutes. Makes 5 dozen.

Mushroom Turnovers

Roquefort Cut-Out Crackers

Dakota Bread ♪

Margaret Scoresby, Mosinee, WI

1 env. active dry yeast
1/2 c. warm water
1/2 c. cottage cheese
1/4 c. honey
1 egg
2 T. oil
1 t. salt
2-1/4 c. bread flour, divided

1/2 c. whole-wheat flour
1/4 c. wheat germ, toasted
1/4 c. rye flour
1/4 c. long-cooking oats, uncooked
2 T. cornmeal
1 egg white, beaten
2 T. sunflower seeds

Combine yeast and warm water (110 to 115 degrees) in a small bowl; let stand 5 minutes. In a large bowl, combine cottage cheese, honey, egg, oil and salt. Beat at medium speed with an electric mixer until blended. Add yeast mixture and 2 cups bread flour, beating until smooth. Gradually stir in whole-wheat flour, wheat germ, rye flour and oats. Add enough remaining bread flour to make a soft dough. Knead dough on a lightly floured surface until smooth and elastic. Place in a greased bowl; cover and let rise one hour or until doubled in bulk. Punch dough down. Shape into one round loaf. Place in a pie plate coated with non-stick vegetable spray and sprinkled with cornmeal. Cover with greased plastic wrap and let dough rise again until doubled in bulk. Brush with egg white and sprinkle with sunflower seeds. Bake at 350 degrees for 35 to 40 minutes. Cool on a wire rack. Makes 6 to 8 servings.

Roquefort Cut-Out Crackers ♪ P. 212

Linda Henderson, Sunset, NC

1 c. all-purpose flour
7 T. crumbled Roquefort or blue cheese
1 egg yolk
4 t. whipping cream

7 T. butter, softened
1/8 t. salt
cayenne pepper to taste
1/2 t. dried parsley

Stir together all ingredients in a large bowl until dough forms. Cover; let stand for 30 minutes. On a floured surface, roll out dough to 1/8-inch thickness. Cut out dough with a round cookie cutter or other desired shape; arrange on an ungreased baking sheet. Bake at 400 degrees for 7 to 9 minutes, just until golden. let cool on baking sheet; store in an airtight container. Makes 2 dozen.

> ✳ **Quick tip**
>
> Grandma's little secret...kneading bread dough is a fun way to get rid of stress! Be sure to knead the dough as long as the recipe states, until the dough is silky smooth. You'll be rewarded with moist, tender bread.

Mom's Raisin Bread ✓

Suzanne Pletsch, Chicago, IL

1 c. milk
1/4 c. margarine
2 t. salt
1/2 c. golden raisins
1 env. active dry rapid-rise yeast
2 T. sugar

1/2 c. warm water
2 eggs, beaten
5 c. all-purpose flour, divided
Optional: beaten egg, milk or softened margarine

Heat milk just to boiling in a small saucepan over low heat; stir in margarine and salt. Add raisins and let cool. Dissolve yeast and sugar in warm water (110 to 115 degrees) in a large saucepan. When milk mixture cools, add it to yeast mixture; stir in eggs. Beat in flour, one cup at a time. When dough gets heavier, start to knead it, adding more flour if too sticky. Knead for about 10 minutes. Place dough in a large greased pan; cover. Set pan in an unheated oven with a pan of hot water placed on rack below it. Let rise for one hour. Punch dough down; let rise for 30 more minutes. Knead dough again; form into 2 loaves and place in 2 greased 8-1/2"x4-1/2" loaf pans. Cover and let rise again for 30 minutes. Brush loaves with egg, milk or margarine, if desired. Bake at 375 degrees for 30 to 45 minutes, until golden. Makes 2 loaves.

Quick tip

Scoop out the centers of small round bread loaves for bread bowls in a snap...extra special for serving hot soup or chili. NO!

Baking Powder Biscuits

Jenna Hord, Mount Vernon, OH

2 c. all-purpose flour
1 T. baking powder
1 t. salt

1/4 c. shortening
3/4 c. milk

In a bowl, sift together flour, baking powder and salt. Cut in shortening with 2 knives or a fork until mixture is as coarse as cornmeal. Add milk; stir just enough to make a soft dough. Turn out dough onto a lightly floured surface; knead for about 30 seconds. Roll out dough 1/2-inch thick. Cut out biscuits with a floured 2-inch round cutter. Place biscuits one inch apart on ungreased baking sheets. Bake at 450 degrees for 12 to 15 minutes, until golden. Makes 15 to 18.

Lucy's Pumpkin-Chocolate Chip Bread ✓

Suzanne Morelli, Foster, RI

15-oz. can pumpkin
4 eggs, beaten
1 c. oil
2 c. sugar
3 c. all-purpose flour

2 t. baking powder
2 t. baking soda
2 t. cinnamon
12-oz. pkg. semi-sweet chocolate chips, divided

In a large bowl, mix together pumpkin, eggs, oil and sugar. Mix in flour, baking powder, baking soda and cinnamon. Stir in half the chocolate chips. Pour batter into a greased and floured Bundt® pan. Sprinkle remaining chocolate chips over batter. Bake at 350 degrees for one hour, or until golden and a toothpick tests clean. Cool and remove from pan. Makes 12 to 16 servings.

Lucy's Pumpkin-Chocolate Chip Bread

Silver Moons

Stone-Ground Corn Rolls
Tina Goodpasture, Meadowview, VA

2 c. milk	1 env. active dry yeast
3/4 c. cornmeal	1/4 c. warm water
1/2 c. sugar	2 eggs, beaten
1/2 c. shortening	6 c. all-purpose flour
1-1/2 t. salt	

Combine milk and cornmeal in a large saucepan; cook over medium heat 15 minutes, or until mixture thickens, stirring frequently. Remove from heat. Add sugar, shortening and salt and stir until blended. Cool slightly. Dissolve yeast in warm water (110 to 115 degrees) in a small bowl. Add eggs and yeast mixture to milk mixture, stirring to blend; gradually stir in flour. Place dough on a lightly floured surface and knead about 5 minutes, until smooth. Shape dough into 2-inch balls; arrange dough balls 2 inches apart on a greased baking sheet. Cover and let rise in a warm place (85 degrees), free from drafts, for one hour, or until double in bulk. Bake at 375 degrees for 15 minutes, or until golden. Makes one dozen.

Molasses Buns
Patsy Leaman, Crockett, TX

1/2 c. boiling water	1/2 t. ground cloves
1/2 c. butter, melted	1/2 t. cinnamon
1/2 c. molasses	1/2 t. nutmeg
1/2 c. sugar	3 c. all-purpose flour
2 t. baking soda	

Mix together all ingredients except flour; set aside until cool. Stir in flour; let stand 20 minutes. Roll dough into balls by tablespoonfuls; place on greased baking sheets. Flatten balls with a spoon; bake at 375 degrees for 20 minutes. Makes about 20 buns.

Silver Moons
Dale Duncan, Waterloo, IA

1 T. sugar	1 c. apple pie filling
1/4 t. cinnamon	4 t. butter, melted
16.3-oz. tube refrigerated large biscuits	Garnish: powdered sugar

In a small bowl, combine sugar and cinnamon; set aside. Separate dough into 8 biscuits. Press each biscuit into a 5-inch circle. Arrange biscuits on greased baking sheets. Place 2 tablespoons pie filling on each circle half. Fold biscuits over filling; seal edges with a fork. Pierce each pie a few times with fork. Brush pies with melted butter and sprinkle with sugar mixture. Bake at 375 degrees for 15 to 20 minutes. Sprinkle with powdered sugar. Serve warm. Makes 8.

Quick tip No!

Eat-it-all bread bowls make hearty soup extra special. Cut the tops off round loaves of bread and hollow out, then rub with olive oil and garlic. Pop bread bowls in the oven at 400 degrees for 10 minutes, or until crusty and golden. Ladle in soup and enjoy!

Grandma Paris' Bambinis

Kristin Santangelo-Winterhoff, Jersey City, NJ

1 c. ricotta cheese
1/2 c. shredded mozzarella cheese
1/4 c. grated Parmesan cheese
10-oz. tube refrigerated large flaky biscuits
20 thin slices pepperoni

Combine cheeses in a bowl; set aside. Halve each biscuit horizontally and gently shape each half into a 4"x2-1/2" oval. Place one pepperoni slice and one tablespoon cheese mixture in the upper half of each oval; fold dough up and over filling, pinching closed. Repeat with remaining ingredients. Arrange on a lightly greased baking sheet; bake at 350 degrees for 20 minutes. Makes 20.

Quick tip

Make a warm loaf of crostini to serve with soup. Slice a loaf of Italian bread into 1/2-inch slices. Brush olive oil over both sides of each slice; sprinkle with coarse salt. Bake in a 300-degree oven for 20 minutes, or until crisp and toasty, turning once.

Cheese Danish Rolls

Diane Vasil, Plano, TX

4 c. all-purpose flour
1 c. shortening, melted
1 c. milk
3 eggs, beaten
5 T. sugar
1/4 c. butter, melted and divided

Combine flour and shortening in a large bowl; mix until crumbly. Heat milk to 120 to 130 degrees. Stir together milk and remaining ingredients except butter; add to flour mixture. Stir 4 to 5 minutes, until dough no longer sticks to the bowl. Refrigerate 3 to 4 hours or overnight. Divide dough into 4 equal parts; roll out each on a floured surface into 11"x7" rectangles. Spoon Cheese Filling down the center of each rectangle; roll up jelly-roll style, starting at short side. Pinch seams together. Arrange on 2 greased baking sheets; brush with 2 tablespoons melted butter. Bake at 375 degrees for 15 to 20 minutes, until golden. Remove from oven; brush with remaining melted butter. Cool and slice. Makes 4 rolls (10 to 12 servings each).

Cheese Filling:

4 8-oz. pkgs. cream cheese, softened
3 eggs, beaten
1-1/2 c. sugar
2 t. vanilla extract

Beat together all ingredients until thick and pudding-like. Makes 6 cups.

Grandma Paris' Bambinis

Red Pepper Muffins

Mile-High Buttermilk Biscuits

Staci Meyers, Montezuma, GA

2 c. all-purpose flour
1 T. baking powder
1 t. salt
1/2 c. shortening, chilled in
  freezer
2/3 to 3/4 c. buttermilk
1/4 c. butter, melted

Mix together flour, baking powder and salt. Cut in shortening with a pastry blender or fork until crumbly. Stir in buttermilk until incorporated and dough leaves sides of bowl. Dough will be sticky. Knead dough 3 to 4 times on a lightly floured surface. Roll out to 1/2-inch thickness, about 2 to 4 passes with a rolling pin. Cut dough with a biscuit cutter, pressing straight down with cutter. Place biscuits on a parchment paper-lined baking sheet. Bake at 500 degrees for 8 to 10 minutes. Brush tops of warm biscuits with melted butter. Makes about one dozen.

Sweet & Spicy Pepper Jelly Cream Cheese

Spread

Holly Child, Parker, CO

8-oz. pkg. cream cheese,
  softened
1/4 c. medium salsa
1/4 c. orange marmalade
assorted crackers

Unwrap cream cheese and place the block on a serving dish. Mix together salsa and marmalade in a bowl; spoon evenly over cream cheese. Serve with assorted crackers. Makes 10 to 12 servings.

Red Pepper Muffins

Personal Pie Pan size to make sand.

Marian Buckley, Fontana, CA

1/2 c. butter
1/2 c. red pepper, finely
  chopped
Optional: 1/3 c. green
  onions, finely chopped
2 eggs, beaten
2/3 c. sour cream
1-1/2 c. all-purpose flour
2 T. sugar
1-1/2 t. baking powder
1/4 t. baking soda
3/4 t. salt
1/2 t. dried basil
1/4 t. dried tarragon

Melt butter in a skillet over medium heat. Cook pepper and onions until tender; let cool. In a bowl, mix eggs and sour cream; stir in pepper mixture. In a separate bowl, combine remaining ingredients. Stir in egg mixture until just moistened. Fill 10 greased muffin cups 2/3 full. Bake at 350 degrees for 20 to 25 minutes, until a toothpick tests clean. Serve warm. Makes 10 muffins.

✳ Quick tip

It's easy to make fresh croutons for salads and soups! Toss bread cubes with olive oil and dried herbs or garlic powder as you like. Toast on a baking sheet at 400 degrees for 5 to 10 minutes, until golden.

Cheesy Batter Bread

Wendy Meadows, Gratis, OH

6-1/3 c. all-purpose flour,
   divided
2 T. sugar
1-1/2 t. salt
2 envs. active dry yeast
2-1/4 c. shredded Cheddar
   cheese, divided

1 c. milk
1 c. water
2 T. butter
1 egg, beaten

Combine 1-1/3 cups flour, sugar, salt, yeast and 2 cups cheese in a large bowl; set aside. Combine milk, water and butter in a saucepan over medium-low heat until very warm (110 to 115 degrees) and butter is almost melted. Gradually stir milk mixture into dry ingredients. Beat with an electric mixer at medium speed for 2 minutes. Add egg and one cup of remaining flour; increase speed to high and beat for 2 minutes. Stir in enough remaining flour with a wooden spoon to make a stiff batter. Cover dough with a tea towel and let rest for 10 minutes. Pour into 2 lightly greased 9"x5" loaf pans. Cover and let rise in a warm draft-free place about one hour, until double in bulk. Sprinkle with remaining cheese; bake at 375 degrees for 25 minutes, or until lightly golden. Remove loaves from pans; cool on wire racks. Makes 2 loaves.

Quick tip

Homemade fruit butter is a delightful way to use a bounty of ripe fruit. It's scrumptious on warm muffins. Try it on waffles or as an ice cream topping too... even give a ribbon-topped jar for a gift anyone would appreciate!

Garlic Bubble Bread

Joanne Grosskopf, Lake in the Hills, IL

16-oz. frozen bread dough,
   thawed
1/4 c. butter, melted
1 T. dried parsley

1 t. garlic powder
1/2 t. garlic salt
Optional: sesame or poppy
   seed

Cut dough into one-inch pieces. Combine butter, parsley, garlic power and garlic salt in a small bowl. Dip dough pieces into butter mixture to coat; layer in a buttered 9"x5" loaf pan. Sprinkle sesame or poppy seed over top, if desired. Cover dough with plastic wrap; let rise in a warm place (85 degrees), free from drafts, about one hour, until double in bulk. Bake at 350 degrees for 30 minutes, or until golden. Cool completely in pan on a wire rack. Makes one loaf.

After-School Doughnuts ♪

Stacey Weichert, Moorhead, MN

2 c. buttermilk
3 eggs, beaten
1/3 c. shortening
2 t. salt
1 t. baking soda
1 t. nutmeg

1/2 t. cinnamon
2 c. sugar
5 c. all-purpose flour,
   divided
oil for deep frying

Blend buttermilk, eggs and shortening together in a large bowl; set aside. In a separate bowl, sift together salt, baking soda, nutmeg, cinnamon, sugar and 2 cups flour; add to buttermilk mixture. Stir in remaining flour; cover and <u>refrigerate overnight</u>. Roll out on a lightly floured surface to 1/3-inch thickness; cut into 3-inch rounds. Heat 3 inches of oil in a heavy stockpot over medium-high <u>heat to 375 degrees</u>. Add doughnuts a few at a time, cooking until golden on both sides, about 2 minutes. Drain on paper towels. <u>Makes 4 to 5 dozen.</u>

After-School Doughnuts

Cinnamon Toast Balls

Maple Nut Twist

Gay Snyder, Deerfield, OH

1/2 c. milk	1/2 c. brown sugar, packed
1/2 c. butter, divided	1/2 c. chopped walnuts
1 env. active dry yeast	1/4 c. maple syrup
1/4 c. warm water	1/2 t. cinnamon
1/3 c. plus 3 T. sugar, divided	1/2 t. maple extract
1-1/2 t. salt	1 c. powdered sugar
2 eggs, beaten	1 to 2 T. water
3-1/4 to 3-1/2 c. plus 2 T. all-purpose flour, divided	

In a saucepan, heat milk and 1/4 cup butter until butter is melted. In a large bowl, dissolve yeast in warm water (110 to 115 degrees); add 3 tablespoons sugar, salt, eggs and 2 cups flour; beat until smooth. Blend in milk mixture. Add 1-1/4 to 1-1/2 cups flour until dough forms; knead until smooth. Cover and let rise in a warm place (85 degrees), away from drafts, 2 hours or until doubled in bulk. In a medium bowl, combine brown sugar, walnuts, remaining sugar, maple syrup, 1/4 cup softened butter, remaining 2 tablespoons flour and cinnamon; set aside. Punch dough down and divide in half; roll out each half into a 14"x8" rectangle. Spread walnut filling over each rectangle. Starting at long side, roll up dough jelly-roll style. With a sharp knife, cut down the center of the jelly-roll lengthwise; twist 2 pieces together to form a rope braid. Turn ends under and shape braid into a ring. Place dough in a greased 9" pie plate and let rise in a warm place one hour or until doubled in bulk. Bake at 350 degrees for 30 minutes, or until golden. Mix together extract, powdered sugar and water; drizzle glaze over warm bread. Serves 16 to 20.

Cinnamon Toast Balls ✓

Martha Stephens, Sibley, LA

12 slices bread, crusts ✓ removed	1 T. cinnamon
1/4 c. butter, melted	1 T. sugar

Tear each slice of bread in half. Roll each half into a ball and place on an ungreased baking sheet. Drizzle balls with melted butter. Combine cinnamon and sugar and sprinkle over balls. Bake at 350 degrees for 5 to 7 minutes. If desired, broil until lightly golden, about 2 minutes. Makes 2 dozen.

> ✳ *Quick tip*
>
> Self-rising flour is handy for quick biscuits. If you're out of it, though, here's an easy substitution. For each cup needed, add 1-1/2 teaspoons baking powder and 1/2 teaspoon salt to a measuring cup, then fill the cup level with all-purpose flour. Mix well before using.

Mother's Rolls
Amy Hansen, Louisville, KY

1 env. active dry yeast	1 T. sugar
3/4 c. warm water	1/4 c. butter, melted
3-1/2 c. biscuit baking mix, divided	additional melted butter

Dissolve yeast in warm water (110 to 115 degrees); let stand 5 minutes. Place 2-1/2 cups biscuit mix in a large bowl; stir in sugar. Add yeast mixture, stirring vigorously. Sprinkle work surface generously with remaining biscuit mix. Place dough on surface and knead 15 to 20 times. Shape heaping tablespoons of dough into balls; arrange on a lightly greased baking sheet. Cover dough with a damp tea towel; set aside in a warm place to rise, about one hour. Brush rolls with melted butter. Bake at 400 degrees for 12 to 15 minutes, until golden. Remove rolls from oven; brush again with melted butter while hot. Makes 15 rolls.

Quick tip

To make a tasty spread for your freshly baked bread or biscuits, just mash your favorite fruit and mix with cottage or ricotta cheese.

Butterhorn Rolls
Francie Stutzman, Dayton, OH

1/2 c. plus 1 T. sugar, divided	1 t. salt
1 c. plus 1/4 c. warm water, divided	3 eggs, lightly beaten
3/4 c. butter, melted and divided	5 c. all-purpose flour

In a large bowl, dissolve yeast and one tablespoon sugar in 1/4 cup warm water (110 to 115 degrees). Add one cup warm water and 1/2 cup butter to yeast mixture. Combine yeast mixture, 1/2 cup sugar, salt and eggs. Add flour, one cup at a time, mixing well. Cover and refrigerate overnight. Remove dough from refrigerator 3 hours before serving. Roll out into a 1/8-inch-thick circle on a heavily floured surface and spread top of dough with remaining melted butter. Cut into wedges like a pie. Roll up each wedge, starting at larger end. Place on a greased baking sheet, cover with a tea towel and let rise in a warm place (85 degrees), away from drafts, until doubled in bulk (about 20 minutes). Remove towel; brush with remaining melted butter. Bake at 375 degrees for 12 to 15 minutes. Makes 16 rolls.

Bran & Raisin Muffins
Jody Pressley, Charlotte, NC

2 c. bran and raisin cereal	1 egg, beaten
1-1/2 c. milk	1/2 c. brown sugar, packed
1-1/2 c. all-purpose flour	2 T. butter, melted
1 t. baking soda	
1/4 t. salt	

Mix cereal with milk; set aside. In a large bowl, combine remaining ingredients; stir in cereal mixture. Fill lightly greased or paper-lined muffin cups about 2/3 full with batter. Bake at 350 degrees for 20 to 25 minutes. Makes one dozen.

Bran & Raisin Muffins

Fresh Strawberry Bread

Holiday Cloverleaf Rolls

Kathy Schroeder, Riverside, CA

4 to 5 c. all-purpose flour, divided	1/2 c. water
1/3 c. sugar	1/2 c. milk
1 t. salt	1/2 c. butter, melted and divided
2 envs. instant dry yeast	2 eggs

In a large mixing bowl, combine one cup flour, sugar, salt and yeast. In a medium saucepan over low heat, heat water, milk and 1/4 cup butter until warm (110 to 115 degrees). Gradually pour liquid into dry ingredients, beating at low speed with an electric mixer. Increase speed to medium; beat 2 minutes, occasionally scraping bowl with rubber spatula. Add eggs and enough flour to make a thick batter. Continue beating 2 minutes, occasionally scraping bowl. With a spoon, stir in enough additional flour to make a soft dough. Turn dough onto a floured surface and knead 10 minutes, or until dough is smooth and elastic. Shape dough into a ball and place in a large greased bowl, turning to coat. Cover with a towel; let rise in a warm place (85 degrees), away from drafts, one hour or until doubled in bulk. Punch down dough in the center, then push edges of dough into center. Turn dough onto a floured surface; cut in half. Cover with a towel 15 minutes. Grease 24 muffin cups. With a sharp knife or kitchen shears, cut half of dough into 36 equal pieces. Shape each piece into a smooth ball. Place 3 balls into each muffin cup. Brush tops with remaining melted butter. Cover with a towel; let rise in a warm place 45 minutes or until doubled in bulk. Repeat with second half of dough. Remove towel from rolls and bake at 400 degrees for 10 to 15 minutes, or until golden. Makes 2 dozen.

Fresh Strawberry Bread *! p 246*

Mary Patenaude, Griswold, CT

3 c. all-purpose flour	4 eggs, beaten
2 c. sugar	2 c. strawberries, hulled and diced
1-1/2 t. cinnamon	Optional: 1-1/4 c. chopped nuts
1 t. baking soda	
1 t. salt	
1 c. oil	

In a bowl, combine flour, sugar, cinnamon, baking soda and salt. In a separate bowl, blend together oil and eggs; fold in strawberries. Gradually add egg mixture into flour mixture; stir until just moistened. Add nuts, if using. Pour into 2 greased and floured 9"x5" loaf pans. Bake at 350 degrees for one hour. Makes 2 loaves.

Quick tip

Make a tasty butter log using fresh herbs from the garden. Blend together butter, chives and shallots, shape into a log and wrap in wax paper; refrigerate until firm. Roll in herbs and serve.

Morning Glory Muffins

Apple Crunch Coffee Cake

Jill Carr, Sutter Creek, CA

1/3 c. butter, softened	1 t. cinnamon
1/3 c. shortening	1/2 t. baking soda
2 c. sugar	1/4 t. salt
2 eggs	1-3/4 c. buttermilk
3 c. all-purpose flour	2 to 3 apples, peeled, cored and sliced
2 t. baking powder	

Beat together butter, shortening and sugar in a large bowl until light and fluffy. Add eggs, one at a time, beating well after each addition; set aside. Stir together flour, baking powder, cinnamon, baking soda and salt in a separate bowl; add to butter mixture alternately with buttermilk. Spread half the batter into a greased 13"x9" baking pan; top with apples. Spread remaining batter over apples; sprinkle with Topping. Bake, uncovered, at 350 degrees for 45 to 55 minutes, until a toothpick inserted in center comes out clean. Serves 12.

Topping:

1 c. all-purpose flour	1 c. brown sugar, packed
1 T. cinnamon	6 T. butter

Stir together flour, brown sugar and cinnamon in a bowl. Cut in butter with a pastry blender or fork until crumbly.

Creamy Ham Croissants

Lisa Johnson, Hallsville, TX

1-1/2 c. cooked ham, diced	12-oz. tube refrigerated crescent rolls
8-oz. pkg. cream cheese, softened	

Mix ham and cream cheese in a bowl; set aside. Unroll and separate crescent rolls; place a spoonful of ham mixture on each. Roll up; place on an ungreased baking sheet. Bake for 15 to 18 minutes at 425 degrees. Makes 8 servings.

Morning Glory Muffins

Violet Leonard, Chesapeake, VA

2 c. all-purpose flour	1/2 c. chopped pecans
1-1/4 c. sugar	3 eggs, beaten
2 t. baking soda	1 c. oil
2 t. cinnamon	1 apple, peeled, cored and shredded
1/2 t. salt	2 t. vanilla extract
2 c. carrots, peeled and grated	
1/2 c. raisins	

In a large bowl, combine flour, sugar, baking soda, cinnamon and salt. Stir in carrots, raisins and pecans. In a separate bowl, combine eggs, oil, apple and vanilla. Add egg mixture to flour mixture; stir until just combined. Spoon into greased or paper-lined muffin cups, filling 3/4 full. Bake at 350 degrees for 15 to 18 minutes, until golden. Makes 1-1/2 dozen.

Quick tip

Savory soup & salad croutons are easy to make. Toss cubes of day-old bread with olive oil, garlic powder, salt and pepper. Spread on a baking sheet in a single layer and bake at 400 degrees for about 10 minutes, until toasty.

Mrs. Claus' Christmas Bread
Francie Stutzman, Dalton, Ohio

O. Zest

1 c. sugar
2 T. butter, softened
1 egg, beaten
2 c. all-purpose flour
1 t. baking powder
1/2 t. baking soda
1/2 t. salt
3/4 c. orange juice ✓
1 c. cranberries, chopped ✓
1/2 c. chopped pecans ✓

Blend sugar, butter and egg together in a large bowl. Add remaining ingredients; mix well and pour into a greased 9"x5" loaf pan. Bake at 350 degrees for 45 to 50 minutes. Makes one loaf.

✳ Quick tip

Treat yourself to crisp savory crackers with your next bowl of soup. Spread saltines with softened butter, then sprinkle with garlic powder, thyme, paprika or another favorite spice. Pop into a 350-degree oven just until golden, 3 to 6 minutes.

Cheddar-Apple Biscuits
Tammie Jones, Lincolnton, NC

1/3 c. brown sugar, packed
2 T. all-purpose flour
1/2 t. cinnamon
10-oz. tube refrigerated
  buttermilk biscuits
1 c. shredded Cheddar
  cheese
2 apples, peeled, cored
  and sliced into rings
1 T. butter, melted

Combine first 3 ingredients in a small bowl; set aside. Press each biscuit into a 3-inch circle. Place on lightly greased baking sheets; sprinkle each with cheese and top with an apple ring. Sprinkle with sugar mixture and drizzle with melted butter. Bake at 350 degrees for 15 minutes, or until golden. Makes 10.

Parmesan Bread Sticks
Mary Murray, Mount Vernon, OH

1/3 c. butter, melted
1 t. dried rosemary,
  crushed
1 clove garlic, minced
2-1/4 c. all-purpose flour
2 T. grated Parmesan
  cheese
1 T. sugar
3-1/2 t. baking powder
1 c. milk

Pour butter into a 13"x9" baking pan, tilting to coat. Sprinkle with rosemary and garlic; set aside. Combine flour, cheese, sugar and baking powder; stir in milk. Turn dough onto a floured surface; knead until smooth. Roll into a 12-inch by 6-inch rectangle; cut into one-inch strips. Twist each strip 6 times; place in butter mixture. Bake at 400 degrees for 20 to 25 minutes. Makes one dozen.

Mrs. Claus' Christmas Bread

Chocolate Rolls

Holiday Ham Balls

Jeanette Lawrence, Vacaville, CA

3 c. biscuit baking mix
1-1/2 c. smoked ham, finely chopped
16-oz. pkg. shredded Cheddar cheese
2/3 c. milk
1/2 c. grated Parmesan cheese
2 T. dried parsley
2 t. spicy mustard

Mix all ingredients thoroughly in a large bowl; shape into one-inch balls. Place about 2 inches apart on lightly greased 15"x10" jelly-roll pans. Bake at 350 degrees for 20 to 25 minutes, until lightly golden. Remove from pans immediately; serve warm. Makes 7 dozen.

Whole-Wheat Pumpkin Bread

Julie Dossantos, Fort Pierce, FL

3-1/2 c. whole-wheat flour
3 c. sugar
2 t. baking soda
1-1/2 t. salt
2 t. cinnamon
2 t. nutmeg
1 c. oil
15-oz. can pumpkin
4 eggs, beaten
2/3 c. water
1-1/2 t. vanilla extract

Spray two 9"x5" loaf pans with non-stick vegetable spray; set aside. In a large bowl, combine flour, sugar, baking soda, salt and spices; mix well. Add oil, pumpkin, eggs, water and vanilla. Beat with an electric mixer on low speed until combined. Pour half of batter into each loaf pan. Bake at 350 degrees for 55 minutes to an hour, until loaves test done with a toothpick inserted in the center. Cool loaves in pans on a wire rack for 15 minutes; turn out of pans. Makes 2 loaves.

Chocolate Rolls

Eleanor Dionne, Beverly, MA

3/4 c. plus 2 T. all-purpose flour
1/4 c. sugar
2 T. baking cocoa
1/4 t. salt
4 eggs
1 c. milk
2 T. butter, melted and slightly cooled
1/2 t. vanilla extract
Garnish: powdered sugar

In a bowl, sift together flour, sugar, cocoa and salt. Set aside. In a separate bowl, beat eggs for one minute. Beat in milk, butter and vanilla. Beat in flour mixture until smooth. Divide batter among 6 greased popover cups or 12 greased muffin cups; set on a 15"x10" jelly-roll pan. Bake at 375 degrees for 50 minutes. Immediately remove to a wire rack. Sprinkle with powdered sugar. Serve immediately. Makes 1-1/2 to 2 dozen.

✳ Quick tip

Dress up a tube of refrigerated bread stick dough. Before baking, brush the dough with a little beaten egg, then sprinkle with sesame seed, grated Parmesan or dried rosemary. A great accompaniment to soup!

Orange Marmalade Bread ✓

Linda Behling, Cecil, PA

1/2 c. butter, softened	2 t. baking powder
1/2 c. brown sugar, packed	1/2 t. baking soda
2 eggs	1 t. salt
10-oz. jar orange ✓ marmalade	1/2 c. orange juice
	1/2 c. chopped nuts
2-3/4 c. all-purpose flour	

Beat together butter and sugar until light and fluffy. Add eggs, one at a time, mixing well. Blend in marmalade; set aside. Combine flour, baking powder, baking soda and salt; add to butter mixture alternately with orange juice. Stir in nuts. Pour into a greased and floured 9"x5" loaf pan. Bake at 350 degrees for about one hour, or until a toothpick inserted in center comes out clean. Cool 15 minutes before removing from pan. Makes one loaf.

Quick tip

Making biscuits and there's no biscuit cutter handy? Try Mom's little trick…just grab a glass tumbler or the open end of a clean, empty soup can.

Lighter-Than-Air Potato Rolls ↓

Linda Cuellar, Riverside, CA

1/2 c. instant mashed potato flakes	1/2 c. hot water
1 t. sugar	1/3 c. cold water
2 T. butter, softened	2 c. biscuit baking mix

Combine potato flakes, sugar, butter and hot water. Stir in cold water and baking mix. Turn dough out onto a floured surface and knead 8 to 10 times. Roll out dough into a 10"x6" rectangle. Cut into 12 squares; place on an ungreased baking sheet. Bake at 450 degrees for about 10 minutes. Makes one dozen.

Herbed Fan Dinner Rolls

Mary Ann Lewandowski, Toledo, OH

1/4 c. butter, melted	11-oz. pkg. refrigerated bread dough
1/2 t. Italian seasoning	

Combine butter and Italian seasoning in a small bowl, stirring well. Roll dough into a 13-inch square. Cut into 4 equal strips. Stack strips on top of each other. Cut strips crosswise into 6 equal stacks. Place each stack, cut-side up, in a greased muffin cup; brush with butter mixture. Cover and let rise in a warm place (85 degrees), free from drafts, 25 minutes or until double in bulk. Bake at 375 degrees for 22 to 25 minutes, until golden. Brush with butter mixture again, if desired. Makes 6.

Lighter-Than-Air Potato Rolls

Pretzel Twists

Cream Biscuits

Jodi Bielawski, Manchester, NH

2 c. all-purpose flour
3 T. sugar
1 T. baking powder
1/2 t. salt
1-1/4 c. whipping cream
1 to 2 T. milk

Combine flour, sugar, baking powder and salt in a large bowl; stir well. Gradually add cream, stirring until mixture forms a soft dough. Shape dough into a ball. Knead dough 6 times on a lightly floured surface; roll out to 1/3-inch thickness. Cut dough into circles with rim of a glass tumbler and place on an ungreased baking sheet. Brush tops of biscuits with milk; bake at 425 degrees for 10 to 15 minutes, until golden. Makes one dozen.

Peppery Biscuit Sticks

Virginia Watson, Scranton, PA

2 c. all-purpose flour
2 T. sugar
2 t. baking powder
1-1/4 t. pepper, divided
1/4 t. baking soda
1/4 t. garlic powder
6 T. butter, chilled
1/2 c. grated Parmesan cheese
1 egg, beaten
1 c. buttermilk, divided

Combine flour, sugar, baking powder, 1/4 teaspoon pepper, baking soda and garlic powder in a large bowl. Cut in butter with a pastry blender or fork until crumbly. Stir in cheese. Make a well in center; set aside. Mix egg and 1/2 cup buttermilk in a small bowl; stir into flour mixture until just moistened. Turn out dough onto a lightly floured surface; knead just until dough holds together. Pat into a 12"x6" rectangle. Brush lightly with additional buttermilk; sprinkle with remaining pepper and press lightly into dough. Cut into 24 strips, each 1/2-inch wide. Arrange one inch apart on ungreased baking sheets. Bake at 450 degrees for 8 minutes, or until golden. Makes 2 dozen.

Pretzel Twists

Marlene Darnell, Newport Beach, CA

2 16-oz. loaves frozen bread dough, thawed
1 egg white, beaten
1 t. water
coarse salt to taste

Divide dough into twenty-four, 1-1/2 inch balls. Roll each ball into a rope 14 inches long. Shape as desired; arrange one inch apart on lightly greased baking sheets. Let rise in a warm place for 20 minutes. Whisk together egg white and water; brush over pretzels. Sprinkle with salt. Place a shallow pan with one inch of boiling water on bottom rack of oven. Bake pretzels on rack above water at 350 degrees for 20 minutes, or until golden. Makes 2 dozen.

Quick tip

Sift flour only when using cake flour. For general baking, just stir the all-purpose flour, spoon lightly into a measuring cup and level off.

Kit's Herbed Bread

Nola Coons, Gooseberry Patch

6 T. butter, softened

2 T. fresh parsley, minced

2 green onions, finely chopped

2 t. fresh basil, minced

1 clove garlic, minced

1/4 t. pepper

1 loaf French bread, halved lengthwise

Combine all ingredients except bread in a small bowl; mix well. Spread on cut sides of bread. Place bread on an ungreased baking sheet. Broil 4 inches from heat for 2 to 3 minutes, or until golden.

Sweet Strawberry Bread *P. 235*

Caroline Schiller, Bayport, NY

3 c. all-purpose flour

1 t. baking soda

1 t. salt

1-1/2 t. cinnamon

2 c. sugar

4 eggs

1-1/2 c. oil

2 c. strawberries, hulled and sliced

1-1/4 c. chopped walnuts

In a large bowl, combine flour, baking soda, salt, cinnamon and sugar. Add eggs, one at a time, beating well after each addition. Stir in oil; mix in remaining ingredients. Divide batter between 2 greased and floured 9"x5" loaf pans. Bake at 350 degrees for one hour. Makes 2 loaves.

This recipe has 1/2 c more oil than P.235 "otherwise recipe"

Honey-Corn Muffins

Lisa Ann Panzino-DiNunzio, Vineland, NJ

1 c. yellow cornmeal

1/4 c. all-purpose flour

1-1/2 t. baking powder

1 egg, beaten

1/3 c. milk

1/4 c. corn

1/4 c. honey

3 T. butter, melted

Combine cornmeal, flour and baking powder; set aside. In a separate bowl, combine egg, milk, corn, honey and butter. Add egg mixture to cornmeal mixture, stirring just enough to moisten. Fill paper-lined muffin cups 2/3 full. Bake at 400 degrees for about 20 minutes. Serve with Honey Butter. Makes 9 to 12 muffins.

Honey Butter:

1 lb. butter, softened

8-oz. jar honey

Combine butter and honey; whip until smooth. Spoon into a covered container; keep refrigerated.

Country Biscuits Supreme

Gretchen Hickman, Galva, IL

2 c. all-purpose flour

4 t. baking powder

2 t. sugar

1/2 t. salt

1/2 t. cream of tartar

1/2 c. shortening

2/3 c. milk

Sift together dry ingredients. Cut in shortening with a pastry blender or fork until crumbly. Add milk; stir just until moistened. Turn dough out onto a lightly floured surface; knead gently for about 30 seconds. Roll out to 1/2-inch thick; cut with a biscuit cutter. Arrange biscuits on an ungreased baking sheet. Bake at 425 degrees for 10 to 12 minutes, until golden. Makes 12 to 15 biscuits.

Sweet Strawberry Bread

Cheese & Garlic Croutons

Mini Cheddar Loaves

Mary King, Ashville, AL

3-1/2 c. biscuit baking mix
2-1/2 c. shredded Cheddar cheese
2 eggs, beaten
1-1/4 c. milk

Combine biscuit mix and cheese in a large bowl. Combine eggs and milk in a separate bowl and beat well; stir egg mixture into cheese mixture. Pour into 2 greased 7"x4" loaf pans or 3 greased 6"x3" loaf pans. Bake at 350 degrees for 40 to 55 minutes, until a toothpick inserted in center comes out clean. Cool completely in pans on wire racks. Makes 2 to 3 loaves.

English Cream Scones

Janis Parr, Ontario, Canada

2 c. all-purpose flour
2 T. sugar
1 T. baking powder
1/2 t. salt
1/4 c. butter
2 eggs
1/3 c. light cream
Garnish: beaten egg white, additional sugar

Combine flour, sugar, baking powder and salt. Cut in butter with 2 knives until mixture resembles coarse cornmeal. In a separate bowl, beat eggs until light; stir in cream. Make a well in the center of flour mixture; slowly add egg mixture. Stir vigorously until dough comes away from the side of the bowl. Pat out dough 3/4-inch thick; cut into squares or triangles. Place on a greased baking sheet. Brush tops with beaten egg white; sprinkle with sugar. Bake at 450 degrees for 12 to 15 minutes. Serve warm. Makes 9 to 12.

Cheese & Garlic Croutons

Kendall Hale, Lynn, MA

1/4 c. butter
1/2 t. dried oregano
1/2 t. dried basil
1/2 t. celery salt
2 cloves garlic, minced
1 T. onion, minced
2 c. whole-wheat bread, cubed
2 T. grated Parmesan cheese

Melt butter in a large skillet. Add seasonings, garlic and onion; cook for about one minute to soften. Stir in bread cubes; sauté until golden and crisp. Toss with cheese until coated. Cool; store in an airtight container. Makes 2 cups.

Quick tip

Add freshly-snipped herbs such as dill weed, basil, or thyme to biscuit dough for delicious variety.

Jack-O'-Lantern Bread ✓
Vickie

2 1-lb. loaves frozen
  bread, dough, thawed

1 T. beaten egg
1-1/2 t. milk

Place both loaves in a bowl. Cover bowl with plastic wrap and let rise until double in bulk, 45 minutes to one hour. Punch dough down, knead loaves together in bowl and shape into a ball. Transfer ball to a greased 15"x12" baking sheet. With greased hands or a lightly floured rolling pin, flatten ball into a 13-inch by 11-inch oval. Cut out eyes and mouth; openings should be at least 1-1/2 to 2 inches wide. (To make small loaves, divide dough into 4 equal pieces and roll into 6-inch by 4-inch ovals; eye and mouth openings should be at least one to 1-1/2 inches wide.) Lift out cut-out dough and bake on another baking sheet or use for decoration. Cover the shaped dough lightly with plastic wrap and let rise until puffy, about 20 minutes. Mix egg with milk in a small bowl; brush over dough. Bake at 350 degrees for 30 to 35 minutes, until golden. Cool on a wire rack. Serve warm or cooled. Serves 10 to 12.

Ham & Cheese Muffins
Leanne Wheless, Borger, TX

1 T. butter

1/3 c. dried, minced onion

8-oz. pkg. shredded
  Cheddar cheese

1-1/2 c. biscuit baking mix

1/2 c. milk

2 eggs

1 c. cooked ham, finely
  chopped

1 t. hickory smoked salt

Melt butter in a skillet. Add onion and cook over low heat until softened; set aside. Combine cheese and biscuit mix in a bowl; stir in milk and eggs just until moistened. Fold in ham, softened onion and salt. Fill 12 greased muffin cups 3/4 full. Bake at 425 degrees for 13 to 15 minutes, until a toothpick comes out clean. Let cool for 5 minutes before removing from muffin cups. Serve warm. Makes one dozen.

Blueberry Puffs •
Kathy Grashoff, Fort Wayne, IN

1 c. buttermilk biscuit ✓
  baking mix

1 c. multi-grain pancake
  mix

2 eggs, beaten

2/3 c. milk

1/3 c. sugar

2 T. butter, melted

1 c. blueberries

Combine the 2 mixes; set aside. Mix eggs, milk, sugar and butter together; add to dry mixes. Fold in blueberries; fill greased muffin cups 3/4 full. Bake at 400 degrees for 15 to 20 minutes; remove to a wire rack to cool. Makes one dozen.

Bette's Pecan Rolls ✓
Michelle Campen, Peoria, IL

1 c. chopped pecans

cinnamon to taste

2 loaves frozen bread
  dough, thawed

5-1/4 oz. pkg. cook & serve
  vanilla pudding mix

2 T. milk

1/2 c. butter, melted

1 c. brown sugar, packed

Sprinkle pecans in the bottom of a greased 13"x9" baking pan; sprinkle with cinnamon. Set aside. Tear dough into 24 walnut-size balls; arrange on top of pecans and set aside. Stir together pudding mix, milk, butter and sugar in a saucepan over low heat until melted; pour over rolls. Cover and refrigerate overnight. Bake at 350 degrees for 30 minutes; invert onto aluminum foil. Makes 2 dozen.

Jack-O'-Lantern Bread

Sandwiches

Nothing pairs better with a steamy bowl of soup than a delicious sandwich. Whether you favor a Toasty Ham & Swiss Stack, a juicy Potluck Beef Sandwich or a simple Tomato Sandwich, it'll taste even better alongside a savory cup of soup. Try a Mexican Hot Dog with a steamy bowl of Cheesy Vegetable Soup, or a Creamy Tuna Melt with some Zucchini & Seashells Soup. From hoagies to croissants, minis to melts, we think you'll find a few new favorites!

Toasty Ham & Swiss Stacks

Toasty Ham & Swiss Stacks ✓
Kristan Weaver, Grove City, OH

2 T. mayonnaise	2 T. olive oil
4 t. Dijon mustard	8 slices rye bread, toasted
2 t. fresh dill, finely chopped	4 slices deli ham
salt and pepper to taste	4 slices Swiss cheese
1 lb. sliced mushrooms	4 thin slices red onion

In a small bowl, whisk together mayonnaise, mustard, dill, salt and pepper; set aside. In a skillet over medium-high heat, sauté mushrooms in oil, stirring occasionally, for 5 minutes, or until liquid evaporates; remove from heat. Spread 4 toast slices with mayonnaise mixture. Layer each slice with ham, mushrooms, cheese and onion. Place on an ungreased baking sheet. Broil under a preheated broiler, about 4 inches from heat, for one to 2 minutes, until lightly golden and cheese is melted. Top with remaining toast slices. Makes 4 servings.

Carolina Chicken Pitas
Sharon Tillman, Hampton, VA

1 onion, chopped	1/2 t. dried oregano
1 lb. boneless, skinless chicken thighs	1/2 c. plain yogurt
1 t. lemon-pepper seasoning	4 rounds pita bread, halved and split

Combine all ingredients except yogurt and pita bread in a slow cooker; mix well. Cover and cook on low setting for 6 to 8 hours. Just before serving, remove chicken from slow cooker and shred with 2 forks. Return shredded chicken to slow cooker; stir in yogurt. Spoon into pita bread. Serves 4.

Fancy Chicken Salad
Andrea Miller, Sugar Land, TX

2 c. cooked chicken, diced	1/2 c. mayonnaise
1/2 c. celery, diced	1/2 t. Worcestershire sauce
1/3 c. seedless grapes, halved	1/2 t. curry powder
2 green onions, sliced	salt and pepper to taste
1/3 c. slivered almonds	

Combine chicken, celery, grapes, onions and almonds. Blend in mayonnaise, Worcestershire sauce and curry powder; add salt and pepper to taste. Serves 4 to 6.

Creamy Tuna Melts ✓
Cindy Atkins, Vancouver, WA

2 to 3 stalks celery, diced	1/4 t. garlic salt
1 onion, diced	1/8 t. sugar
12-oz. can tuna, drained	4 English muffins, split and toasted
1/2 c. cottage cheese	8 slices American cheese
1/2 c. mayonnaise	

In a skillet sprayed with non-stick vegetable spray, sauté celery and onion until tender. Add tuna, cottage cheese, mayonnaise, garlic salt and sugar to skillet. Mix well, breaking up tuna. Cook over low heat until warmed through, stirring frequently; remove from heat. Place toasted muffins cut-side up on a broiler pan. Spread with tuna mixture; top with cheese slices. Broil until cheese melts; serve immediately. Serves 8.

Turkey-Veggie Bagels •

April Jacobs, Loveland, CO

4 onion bagels, sliced in half

4 leaves romaine lettuce

8 slices deli smoked turkey

1 cucumber, thinly sliced

2 to 4 radishes, thinly sliced

1 to 2 carrots, peeled and shredded

1/4 c. cream cheese with chives and onions

Arrange 4 bagel halves on a serving tray. Place a lettuce leaf on each; top with turkey, cucumber, radish and carrot. Spread cream cheese on top halves of bagels; place on bottom halves. Makes 4 sandwiches.

Grilled Cuban Sandwiches

Gladys Kielar, Perrysburg, OH

1 loaf French bread, halved lengthwise

2 T. Dijon mustard

6-oz. pkg, thinly sliced Swiss cheese

6-oz. pkg. sliced deli ham

8 dill pickle sandwich slices

Spread cut sides of bread with mustard. Arrange half of cheese and ham on bottom half of bread; top with pickle slices. Repeat with remaining cheese and ham; cover with top half of bread. Slice into quarters. Arrange sandwiches in a lightly greased skillet; place a heavy skillet on top of sandwiches. Cook over medium-high heat 2 minutes on each side, or until golden and cheese is melted. Makes 4 sandwiches.

Greek Chicken Pitas

Peggy Pelfrey, Fort Riley, KS

1 onion, diced

3 cloves garlic, minced

1 lb. boneless, skinless chicken breasts, cut into strips

1 t. lemon-pepper seasoning

1/2 t. dried oregano

1/4 t. allspice

1/4 c. plain yogurt

1/4 c. sour cream

1/2 c. cucumber, peeled and diced

4 rounds pita bread, halved and split

Optional: sliced cucumber, sliced red onion, feta cheese, fresh oregano

Place onion and garlic in a slow cooker; set aside. Sprinkle chicken with seasonings; place in slow cooker. Cover and cook on high setting for 6 hours. Stir together yogurt, sour cream and cucumber in a small bowl; chill. Fill pita halves with chicken and drizzle with yogurt sauce. Garnish as desired. Serves 4.

*

Quick tip

Try something easy for brown-bag lunches... roll any combination of cheese, deli meat and veggies in a tortilla. Even a kid-friendly peanut butter & jelly wrap tastes terrific!

Turkey-Veggie Bagels

Pepper Steak Sammies

Pepper Steak Sammies

Vickie

1 to 1-1/4 lbs. beef sirloin
  or ribeye steak
2 green peppers, thinly
  sliced
1 onion, sliced
4 cloves garlic, minced and
  divided
1 T. vegetable oil
salt and pepper to taste
1/3 c. butter, softened
4 French rolls, split and
  toasted

Grill or broil steak to desired doneness; set aside. Sauté green peppers, onion and 2 cloves garlic in hot oil in a skillet over medium heat until crisp-tender; drain. Slice steak thinly; add to skillet and heat through. Sprinkle with salt and pepper. Blend butter and remaining garlic in a small bowl; spread over cut sides of rolls. Spoon steak mixture onto bottom halves of rolls; cover with tops. Makes 4 sandwiches.

Mark's Egg Salad Sandwiches

Mark's Egg Salad Sandwiches

Connie Herek, Bay City, MI

6 eggs, hard-boiled, peeled
  and chopped
1/3 c. celery, finely
  chopped
1/3 c. onion, finely
  chopped
3 to 4 T. mayonnaise-type
  salad dressing
1 to 2 t. mustard
1 t. Worcestershire sauce
1/2 t. salt
1/4 t. pepper
1/2 t. dry mustard
1 T. dill weed
1 loaf sliced bread

Mix all ingredients except bread in a small bowl; refrigerate about one hour. Spread on half of bread slices; top with remaining bread slices. Makes 6 to 8 sandwiches.

✳ Quick tip

Jazz up your sandwiches with this super-simple veggie spread! Blend one cup cottage cheese, 1/4 cup plain Greek yogurt, one tablespoon minced onion, one teaspoon dried parsley and 1/4 teaspoon dill weed.

Rosemary-Dijon Chicken Croissants

Caesar Focaccia Sandwich ❧

Wendy Ball, Battle Creek, MI

2 c. mixed salad greens

1/4 c. Caesar salad dressing

8-inch round focaccia bread or round loaf, halved horizontally

4 slices Cheddar cheese

1/4 lb. deli ham, thinly shaved

1/4 lb. deli turkey, thinly shaved

1 tomato, sliced

1 slice red onion, separated into rings

Garnish: pickles, potato chips

Toss salad greens with salad dressing in a small bowl; set aside. Layer the bottom half of focaccia with greens mixture and remaining ingredients except garnish. Add the top half of focaccia; cut into halves or quarters. Serve with pickles and chips on the side. Serves 2 to 4.

Rosemary-Dijon Chicken Croissants

Jo Ann

3 c. cooked chicken breast, chopped

1/3 c. green onions, chopped

2 T. toasted almonds, coarsely chopped

1/4 c. plain yogurt

1/4 c. mayonnaise

1 t. fresh rosemary, chopped

1 t. Dijon mustard

1/8 t. salt

1/8 t. pepper

Optional: leaf lettuce

10 mini croissants, split

Combine all ingredients except lettuce and croissants in a large bowl; mix well. Arrange lettuce leaves inside croissants, if desired; spread with chicken mixture. Makes 10 mini sandwiches.

Strawberry Patch Sandwich p.294

Shelley Turner, Boise, ID

2 slices whole-wheat bread or banana bread

1 T. creamy peanut butter

1 T. cream cheese, softened

2 strawberries, hulled and sliced

1 t. honey

Spread one slice of bread with peanut butter. Spread remaining slice with cream cheese. Arrange strawberry slices in a single layer over peanut butter. Drizzle honey over berries; top with remaining bread slice. Makes one sandwich.

Caesar Focaccia Sandwich

Easy French Dip Sandwiches

Easy French Dip Sandwiches

Kathy White, Cato, NY

4 lbs. stew beef, cubed
2 onions, halved
4 cloves garlic
2 10-1/2 oz. cans beef broth
4 c. water
4 t. beef bouillon granules
sandwich buns, split

Combine all ingredients except buns in a slow cooker. Cover and cook on low setting for 8 to 10 hours. Discard onions and garlic. Remove beef to a bowl and shred; spoon onto buns. Serve with beef juices from slow cooker for dipping. Serves 18 to 20.

Avocado Egg Salad Sandwiches

Crystal Bruns, Iliff, CO

6 eggs, hard-boiled, peeled and chopped
2 avocados, peeled, pitted and cubed
1/2 c. red onion, minced
1/3 c. mayonnaise
3 T. sweet pickles, chopped
1 T. mustard
salt and pepper to taste
12 slices bread

Mash eggs with a fork in a bowl until crumbly. Add remaining ingredients except bread slices. Gently mix together until blended. Spread egg mixture evenly over 6 bread slices. Top with remaining bread slices. Makes 6 sandwiches.

Herb Garden Sandwiches

Lynda Robson, Boston, MA

8-oz. pkg. cream cheese, softened
1/2 c. fresh herbs, finely chopped, such as parsley, watercress, basil, chervil, chives
1 t. lemon juice
1/8 t. hot pepper sauce
8 slices whole-wheat bread, crusts removed
paprika to taste

Combine all ingredients except bread and paprika. Spread cream cheese mixture evenly over half of bread slices. Sprinkle with paprika. Top with remaining bread slices; slice diagonally into quarters. Makes 16 mini sandwiches.

Regina's Stuffed Pitas

Regina Vining, Warwick, RI

1/2 lb. deli roast beef, cut into thin strips
2 c. romaine lettuce, shredded
1 c. carrot, peeled and shredded
1 c. cucumber, thinly sliced
1/2 c. red onion, thinly sliced
1/3 c. crumbled feta cheese
3 T. pine nuts, toasted
4 pita rounds, halved and split
2 T. mayonnaise
2 T. milk
1 T. cider vinegar

Stir together beef and next 6 ingredients. Spoon mixture evenly inside pita halves. Whisk together remaining ingredients. Lightly drizzle over each pita filling. Makes 4 sandwiches.

Crab & Broccoli Rolls

Crab & Broccoli Rolls

Jane Moore, Haverford, PA

6-oz. can flaked crabmeat, drained

10-oz. pkg. frozen chopped broccoli, cooked, drained and cooled

1/4 c. mayonnaise

1/2 c. shredded Swiss cheese

8-oz. tube refrigerated crescent rolls, separated

Combine crabmeat, broccoli, mayonnaise and cheese; spread about 2 tablespoons on each crescent. Roll up crescent roll-style; arrange on a lightly greased baking sheet. Bake at 375 degrees for 18 to 20 minutes. Makes 8 rolls.

Santa Fe Sandwiches

Deanne Birkestrand, Minden, NE

6 hoagie buns, split in half horizontally

1/2 c. mayonnaise

1/2 c. sour cream

1/2 t. chili powder

1/2 t. cumin

1/4 t. salt

6 tomatoes, sliced

8-oz. pkg. sliced cooked turkey

1/2 c. sliced black olives

1/3 c. green onion, sliced

3 avocados, peeled, pitted and sliced

8-oz. pkg. shredded Cheddar cheese

Garnish: shredded lettuce, salsa

Arrange hoagie buns cut-side up on an ungreased baking sheet; set aside. Combine mayonnaise and next 4 ingredients; spread over hoagie buns. Evenly layer buns with tomatoes, turkey, olives, onion, avocados and cheese. Bake at 350 degrees for 15 minutes. Slice each sandwich in half to serve; garnish with shredded lettuce and salsa. Makes 12 open-faced sandwiches.

Santa Fe Sandwiches

Debbie's Savory Roast Sandwiches

Debbie Fuls, Pennsylvania Furnace, PA

3 to 4-lb. beef or pork roast

14-oz. bottle catsup

1/2 c. taco sauce

1 onion, chopped

2 cloves garlic, pressed

2 T. brown sugar, packed

2 T. Worcestershire sauce

1 T. vinegar

1/8 t. dried oregano

1/8 t. dry mustard

1/8 t. pepper

10 to 12 hard rolls, split

Place roast in a 5 to 6-quart slow cooker. Mix together catsup and remaining ingredients except rolls; pour over roast. Cover and cook on low setting for 5 to 6 hours. Remove roast from slow cooker; shred with 2 forks. Serve on rolls. Makes 10 to 12 sandwiches.

Giant Stuffed Sandwich

Giant Stuffed Sandwich

Helen Williams, Heath, OH

1/2 c. quick-cooking oats, uncooked

1/2 c. boiling water

2 T. butter

16-oz. pkg. hot roll mix ✓

3/4 c. very warm water (110 to 115 degrees)

2 eggs, beaten

1/2 c. mayonnaise

1/4 c. coarse mustard

9-oz. pkg. sliced deli honey ham

6-oz. pkg. sliced deli roast turkey

6-oz. pkg. sliced deli roast *beef* chicken

1 to 2 tomatoes, thinly sliced

1 red onion, thinly sliced

8 slices Cheddar cheese

Garnish: shredded lettuce

deli roast beef

Combine oats, boiling water and butter in a large bowl; let stand for 5 minutes. Dissolve yeast from roll mix in warm water; add to oat mixture. Stir well; mix in eggs. Add flour from roll mix; blend well. Form into a 10-inch circle on a greased 12" pizza pan. Cover; let rise for 25 minutes, until double. Bake at 350 degrees for 25 minutes. Cool on a wire rack; cut in half horizontally. Whisk together mayonnaise and mustard; spread over cut sides. Assemble sandwich with remaining ingredients and cut into wedges. Serves 8 to 12.

Reuben Sandwich

Linda Webb, Delaware, OH

2 slices corned beef

1 slice Swiss cheese

2 slices dark rye or pumpernickel bread

4 T. sauerkraut

1-1/2 T. Thousand Island salad dressing

3 T. butter

Place one slice each corned beef and cheese on a slice of bread. Top with sauerkraut and dressing. Add a second slice of corned beef and remaining bread. Melt butter in a skillet over medium heat; add sandwich to pan. Grill each side until cheese melts and bread is toasted. Makes one sandwich.

Yummy Blue Cheese Burgers

Lynn Daniel, Portage, MI

2 lbs. ground beef

Cajun seasoning to taste

1 c. half-and-half

1 clove garlic, finely minced

1 t. dried rosemary

1 t. dried basil

4-oz. container crumbled blue cheese

6 kaiser rolls, split, toasted and buttered

Optional: sliced mushrooms, sliced onion, butter

Shape beef into 6 patties; sprinkle with Cajun seasoning. Grill patties over medium-high heat, 350 to 400 degrees, to desired doneness, turning to cook on both sides. Combine half-and-half, garlic and herbs in a saucepan. Bring to a boil; reduce heat and simmer until mixture is thickened and reduced by half. Add blue cheese; stir just until melted. Place burgers on bottom halves of rolls; spoon sauce over burgers. If desired, sauté mushrooms and onion in butter until tender; spoon onto burgers. Top with remaining roll halves. Makes 6 sandwiches.

Roast Beef & Pepper Panini

Jennie Gist, Gooseberry Patch

8 thick slices Italian bread

8 slices deli roast beef

4 slices mozzarella cheese

8-oz. jar roasted red peppers, drained and chopped

2 T. green olives with pimentos, diced

1 T. olive oil

Top 4 slices of bread with roast beef, cheese, peppers and olives; add remaining bread slices. Brush oil on both sides of sandwiches. Heat a large skillet over medium heat; add sandwiches. Cook 2 to 3 minutes on each side, until golden and cheese is melted. Slice sandwiches in half to serve. Makes 4 sandwiches.

Game-Day Sandwich ♪

Yvonne Coleman, Statesville, NC

3 T. mayonnaise
1 T. mustard
1-lb. round loaf Hawaiian-style bread
1/4 lb. sliced deli turkey ✓
1/4 lb. sliced deli roast beef ✓
3 slices Swiss cheese

3 lettuce leaves
1/4 lb. sliced deli ham ✓
6 slices bacon, crisply cooked ✓
3 slices Cheddar cheese
6 slices tomato

Mix mayonnaise and mustard together. Cut bread horizontally into 3 layers. Spread half of mayonnaise mixture on the bottom layer. Add turkey, roast beef, Swiss cheese and lettuce. Cover with middle bread layer; spread with remaining mayonnaise mixture. Add ham, bacon, Cheddar cheese and tomato. Top with remaining bread layer. Cut into 6 to 8 slices. Makes 6 to 8 servings.

Quick tip

Give any sandwich a happy face...the kids will love 'em! Arrange olive slices for eyes, a banana pepper nose, carrot crinkle ears and parsley hair.

Chicken Salad Sandwiches ♪

Susan Smith, London, OH

1-1/4 lbs. chicken breast, cooked and diced
1 c. celery, thinly sliced
1 c. seedless red grapes, halved
1/2 c. raisins
1/2 c. plain yogurt
1/4 c. mayonnaise

2 T. shallots, chopped
2 T. fresh tarragon, chopped
1/2 t. salt
1/8 t. white pepper
6 whole-wheat buns, split
lettuce leaves

Combine chicken, celery, grapes and raisins in a large bowl; set aside. Blend together yogurt, mayonnaise, shallots, tarragon, salt and pepper in a small bowl. Add yogurt mixture to chicken mixture; stir gently to coat. Divide mixture evenly among buns. Place lettuce leaves over chicken mixture and place tops on buns. Makes 6 sandwiches.

Stuffed Pockets ♪

Kathy Bradshaw, Fargo, ND

3 whole pita rounds, cut in half
lettuce leaves
6 slices deli ham, thinly sliced
6 slices Cheddar cheese
1 red onion, sliced into rings

1 tomato, sliced
ranch-style salad dressing to taste
4 slices bacon, crisply cooked and crumbled

Slightly open pita halves and stuff with lettuce, ham, cheese, onion and tomato. Top with salad dressing and crumbled bacon. Makes 6 sandwiches.

Game-Day Sandwich

Farmhands' Stuffed Sandwich

Farmhands' Stuffed Sandwich ✒

Barbara Shultis, South Egremont, MA

1 round loaf hearty bread
2 T. Italian salad dressing
8 slices provolone cheese, divided
1/8 lb. deli salami, sliced
2-1/4 oz. can sliced black olives, drained
1/2 lb. mild Italian pork sausage links, browned and sliced
1 thick slice red onion

6 T. pizza sauce
7 pepperoncini, drained and sliced
1/4 lb. deli turkey, sliced
4-oz. jar sun-dried tomatoes in oil, drained and sliced
2 T. shredded Parmesan cheese
Optional: 2 T. garlic, pressed

Slice off top quarter of loaf; hollow out top and bottom of loaf. Brush salad dressing inside bottom half. Layer with half of cheese slices; layer on remaining ingredients in order listed, ending with remaining cheese slices. Replace top half of loaf. Place on an ungreased baking sheet; set another baking sheet on top. Weight with a heavy object such as a food can or a cast-iron skillet. Let stand 30 minutes to one hour. Cut into wedges to serve. Serves 8.

Chili Crescent Cheese Dogs

Jen Martineau, Delaware, OH

8-oz. tube refrigerated crescent rolls
8 hot dogs

1 c. shredded Cheddar cheese
1 c. chili

Separate crescent rolls into triangles. Place one hot dog in middle of each dough triangle; sprinkle each with cheese. Spoon chili over cheese. Fold dough corners inward to partially cover each hot dog, pressing ends to seal. Arrange on an ungreased baking sheet. Bake at 425 degrees for 10 to 12 minutes or until crescents are golden and hot dogs are heated through. Serves 8.

Tex-Mex Chili Dogs

Stacie Avner, Delaware, OH

1-lb. pkg. hot dogs
2 15-oz. cans chili without beans
10-3/4 oz. can Cheddar cheese soup
4-oz. can chopped green chiles

10 hot dog buns, split
Garnish: chopped onions, crushed corn chips, shredded Cheddar cheese

Place hot dogs in a slow cooker. Combine chili, soup and green chiles in a large bowl; pour over hot dogs. Cover and cook on low setting for 4 to 5 hours. Serve hot dogs in buns; top with chili mixture and garnish as desired. Serves 10.

Quick tip

Save the plastic liners when you toss out empty cereal boxes. They make terrific wrappers for sandwiches that will go into lunchboxes.

Slow-Cooked Pulled Pork

Tina Goodpasture, Meadowview, VA

1 T. oil
3-1/2 to 4-lb. boneless pork shoulder roast, tied
10-1/2 oz. can French onion soup
1 c. catsup

1/4 c. cider vinegar
2 T. brown sugar, packed
24 slices Texas toast or 12 sandwich rolls, split

Heat oil in a skillet over medium heat. Add roast and brown on all sides; remove to a large slow cooker and set aside. Mix soup, catsup, vinegar and brown sugar; pour over roast. Cover and cook on low setting for 8 to 10 hours, until roast is fork-tender. Remove roast to a platter; discard string and let stand for 10 minutes. Shred roast, using 2 forks; return to slow cooker and stir. Spoon meat and sauce onto bread slices or rolls. Makes 12 sandwiches.

Slow-Cooked Pulled Pork

Bacon Quesadillas

Edward Kielar, Perrysburg, OH

1 c. shredded Colby Jack cheese
1/4 c. bacon bits
1/4 c. green onion, thinly sliced
Optional: 4-1/2 oz. can green chiles

Optional: 1/4 c. red or green pepper, chopped
4 6-inch flour tortillas
Garnish: sour cream, salsa

Combine cheese, bacon bits and onion in a small bowl; add chiles and peppers, if desired. Sprinkle mixture equally over one half of each tortilla. Fold tortillas in half; press lightly to seal edges. Arrange on a lightly greased baking sheet. Bake at 400 degrees for 8 to 10 minutes until edges are lightly golden. Top with a dollop of sour cream and salsa. Serves 4.

Quick tip

To freshen a loaf of bread that's beginning to go stale, tuck a stalk of celery into the bread bag overnight.

Bacon Quesadillas

Herbed Shrimp Tacos

Herbed Shrimp Tacos

Lori Vincent, Alpine, UT

juice of 1 lime
1/2 c. plus 1 T. fresh cilantro, chopped and divided
1/2 t. salt
1/2 t. pepper
1/8 t. dried thyme
1/8 t. dried oregano
1 lb. uncooked medium shrimp, peeled and cleaned

1/2 c. radishes, shredded
1/2 c. cabbage, shredded
1/2 c. red onion, chopped
Optional: 2 T. oil
10 6-inch flour tortillas, warmed
Optional: guacamole, lettuce

Combine lime juice, one tablespoon cilantro, salt, pepper and herbs in a large plastic zipping bag; mix well. Add shrimp; seal bag and refrigerate at least one hour. Combine radishes, cabbage, onion and remaining 1/2 cup cilantro in a bowl; set aside. Thread shrimp onto skewers; grill over medium-high heat until pink and cooked through, or heat oil in a skillet over medium heat and sauté shrimp until done. Spoon into warm tortillas with cabbage mixture; serve with guacamole and lettuce, if desired. Serves 10.

Quick tip

Try something new...grilled cheese croutons! Make grilled cheese sandwiches as usual, then slice them into small squares. Toss into a bowl of creamy tomato soup. Delicious!.

Taco Joes

Sherry Cress, Salem, IN

3 lbs. ground beef, browned and drained
16-oz. can refried beans
10-oz. can enchilada sauce
1-1/4 oz. pkg. taco seasoning mix
16-oz. jar salsa

25 hot dog buns, split
Garnish: shredded Cheddar cheese, shredded lettuce, chopped tomatoes, sour cream

Place ground beef in a slow cooker. Stir in beans, enchilada sauce, taco seasoning and salsa. Cover and cook on low setting for 4 to 6 hours. To serve, fill each bun with 1/3 cup beef mixture and garnish as desired. Serves 25.

The Ultimate Shrimp Sandwich

Karen Pilcher, Burleson, TX

3/4 lb. cooked shrimp, chopped
1/4 c. green pepper, chopped
1/4 c. celery, chopped
1/4 c. cucumber, chopped
1/4 c. tomato, diced
1/4 c. green onion, chopped

1/4 c. mayonnaise
Optional: hot pepper sauce to taste
6 split-top rolls, split and lightly toasted
2 T. butter, softened
1 c. shredded lettuce

Combine shrimp and next 6 ingredients; add hot pepper sauce, if desired, and toss well. Set aside. Spread rolls evenly with butter; divide lettuce among rolls. Top with shrimp mixture. Makes 6.

Mexican Burgers

Mushroom & Steak Hoagies ♪
Mandy Sheets, Homedale, ID

1 c. water
1/3 c. soy sauce
1-1/2 t. garlic powder
1-1/2 t. pepper
1-lb. beef round steak, cut into 1/4-inch strips
1 onion, sliced
1 green pepper, thinly sliced
4-oz. can mushroom stems and pieces, drained
2 c. shredded mozzarella cheese
6 hoagie buns, split

Whisk together water, soy sauce, garlic powder and pepper in a bowl; add steak, turning to coat. Cover and refrigerate overnight. Drain and discard marinade; brown steak in a large skillet over medium-high heat. Add onion, green pepper and mushrooms; sauté 8 minutes, or until tender. Reduce heat; top with cheese. Remove from heat; stir until cheese melts and meat is coated. Spoon onto buns to serve. Serves 6.

Mexican Burgers ♪
Stacie Avner, Delaware, OH

1 avocado, peeled, pitted and diced
1 plum tomato, diced
2 green onions, chopped
1 to 2 t. lime juice
1-1/4 lbs. ground beef
1 egg, beaten
3/4 c. to 1 c. nacho-flavored tortilla chips, crushed
1/4 c. fresh cilantro, chopped
1/2 t. chili powder
1/2 t. ground cumin
salt and pepper to taste
1-1/4 c. shredded Pepper Jack cheese
5 hamburger buns, split

Combine avocado, tomato, onions and lime juice; mash slightly and set aside. Combine ground beef, egg, chips and seasonings in a large bowl. Form into 5 patties. Grill over medium-high heat to desired doneness, turning to cook on both sides. Sprinkle cheese over burgers; grill until melted. Place burgers on bottoms of buns; top with avocado mixture and bun tops. Makes 5 sandwiches.

> ✳ **Quick tip**
>
> A fruity cream cheese spread tastes delicious on sandwiches. Just combine one 8-ounce package of softened cream cheese with 1/4 cup apricot preserves. Stir until smooth. So delicious on turkey or ham sandwiches!

Mushroom & Steak Hoagies

Turkey Panini

Turkey Panini
Sue Steadman, Phoenix, AZ

1/4 c. whole-berry cranberry sauce

2 to 3 t. prepared horseradish

2 T. mayonnaise

4 1/2-inch thick large slices ciabatta bread

4 3/8-inch thick slices cooked turkey breast or deli turkey

salt and pepper to taste

4 slices provolone cheese

4 slices bacon, crisply cooked

1-1/2 T. olive oil

Optional: mixed salad greens

Combine cranberry sauce and horseradish, stirring well. Spread mayonnaise on one side of each slice of bread. Spread cranberry-horseradish sauce on 2 slices of bread; top each sandwich with 2 turkey slices and sprinkle with salt and pepper. Arrange 2 cheese slices on each sandwich; top with 2 bacon slices. Cover with tops of bread, mayonnaise-side down. Brush tops and bottoms of sandwiches with olive oil. Cook on a panini press 3 minutes or until cheese begins to melt and bread is toasted. Garnish with mixed salad greens, if desired. Serve hot. Makes 2 sandwiches.

Quick tip

Easiest-ever sandwiches for a get-together...a big platter of cold cuts, a basket of fresh breads and a choice of condiments so guests can make their own. Add cups of hot soup plus cookies for dessert...done!

Hula Ham Wraps
Nancy Wise, Little Rock, AR

3/4 lb. deli ham, sliced into strips

20-oz. can pineapple tidbits, drained

2 carrots, peeled and shredded

1 head napa cabbage, shredded

1 c. sour cream

1/4 c. white wine vinegar

1 t. salt

1/4 t. pepper

Optional: 1 t. caraway seed

12 10-inch flour tortillas

Combine ham, pineapple, carrots and cabbage in a large bowl; set aside. In a separate bowl, whisk together sour cream, vinegar, salt, pepper and caraway seed, if desired. Pour over ham mixture; toss. Divide among tortillas and roll into wraps. Makes 12 wraps.

Raspberry-Dijon Baguettes
Deborah Lomax, Peoria, IL

1 baguette, sliced

Dijon mustard to taste

raspberry jam to taste

4 boneless, skinless chicken breasts, grilled and sliced

2 c. arugula leaves

Optional: red onion slices

Spread 4 slices of baguette with mustard. Top remaining slices with raspberry jam. Arrange a layer of grilled chicken over mustard; top with arugula and onion, if desired. Cover with remaining baguette slices. Serves 4.

Sandwiches

Vickie's Shredded Chicken Sandwiches

Vickie

4 T. olive oil

4 boneless, skinless chicken breasts

1 onion, chopped

10-3/4 oz. can cream of mushroom soup

1 c. chicken broth

2 t. soy sauce

2 t. Worcestershire sauce

1/2 c. sherry or chicken broth

salt and pepper to taste

8 sandwich buns, split

Optional: pickle slices, lettuce leaves

Heat oil in a skillet over medium-high heat. Brown chicken for 5 minutes on each side. Place chicken in a slow cooker; set aside. Add onion to skillet; sauté until golden. Add soup, broth, sauces, sherry or broth, salt and pepper to skillet; stir well and pour over chicken in slow cooker. Cover and cook on low setting for 6 to 8 hours. Shred chicken with a fork; spoon onto buns. Garnish with pickles and lettuce, if desired. Makes 8 sandwiches.

✳ Quick tip

Get ready for spur-of-the-moment picnics on sunny days...tuck a basket filled with picnic supplies into the car trunk along with a quilt to sit on. One stop at a farmers' market for food and you'll be dining in sunshine!

Weekend Treat Burgers

Marie Warner, Jennings, FL

2/3 c. shredded provolone cheese

1/2 c. green pepper, diced

1/2 c. onion, chopped

salt and pepper to taste

2 lbs. ground beef chuck

4 sesame seed Kaiser rolls, split

Toss together cheese, green pepper, onion, salt and pepper in a large bowl. Add ground beef; mix well, and form into 4 patties. Fry in a skillet over medium-high heat for 4 to 5 minutes on each side, until desired doneness. Serve on rolls. Serves 4.

Grilled Ham Panini

Tina Goodpasture, Meadowview, VA

2 slices sourdough bread

1 T. mayonnaise

6 slices deli smoked ham

2 slices tomato

1 slice American cheese

Spread both slices of bread with mayonnaise on one side. Top one slice with ham, tomato, cheese and remaining bread slice. Spray a griddle or skillet with non-stick vegetable spray. Place ham sandwich on griddle; set a bacon press or other weight on top. Cook sandwich, turning once, over medium heat for about 5 minutes or until lightly golden on both sides. Makes one sandwich.

Vickie's Shredded Chicken Sandwiches

Zesty Italian Beef

Zesty Italian Beef

Jennifer Maxey, Mount Vernon, IL

3-lb. beef chuck roast, quartered
1 to 2 T. oil
2-oz. pkg. zesty Italian salad dressing mix
12-oz. can beer or non-alcoholic beer
1 onion, chopped
6 to 7 pepperoncini peppers, chopped
6 to 8 sandwich buns, split

Brown roast in oil in a skillet over medium heat; place into a slow cooker. Sprinkle with dressing mix; pour beer over top. Add onion and peppers. Cover and cook on high setting for 5 to 6 hours, until meat shreds easily with a fork. Spoon onto sandwich buns. Makes 6 to 8 sandwiches.

Tomato Sandwiches

Diane Long, Delaware, OH

3 tomatoes, thickly sliced
10 sprigs watercress
1 red onion, sliced
1 green pepper, sliced
10 slices pumpernickel bread
salt and pepper to taste
mayonnaise to taste

Place 2 tomato slices, 2 sprigs of watercress, a slice of onion and 2 slices of green pepper on half of the bread slices. Sprinkle with salt and pepper. Spread mayonnaise over remaining bread slices and top sandwiches. Makes 5 sandwiches.

Grilled Veggie Sandwich

Wendy Jacobs, Idaho Falls, ID

1/4 c. balsamic vinegar
2 T. olive oil
1 T. fresh basil, chopped
2 t. molasses
1-1/2 t. fresh thyme, chopped
1/4 t. salt
1/4 t. pepper
3 zucchini, sliced
1 yellow pepper, coarsely chopped
2 red peppers, coarsely chopped
1 onion, sliced
16-oz. loaf French bread
3/4 c. crumbled feta cheese
2 T. mayonnaise
1/4 c. freshly grated Parmesan cheese

Whisk together vinegar, olive oil, basil, molasses, thyme, salt and pepper. Place zucchini, peppers and onion in a large plastic zipping bag. Add vinegar mixture; seal and refrigerate 2 hours, turning bag occasionally. Remove vegetables from bag and set aside; reserve marinade. Slice bread loaf in half horizontally and brush 3 or 4 tablespoons reserved marinade over inside of bread. Lightly coat grill with non-stick vegetable spray. Add vegetables and grill 5 minutes, basting occasionally with remaining marinade. Turn vegetables, baste and grill 2 more minutes. Place bread, cut-side down on grill and grill 3 minutes or until vegetables are tender and bread is toasted. Combine feta cheese and mayonnaise; spread evenly over cut sides of bread. Layer grilled vegetables on bottom half of bread; add Parmesan cheese and top with remaining bread. Slice into 8 sections. Makes 8 sandwiches.

Philly Cheesesteak Sandwiches

Amy Michalik, Norwalk, IA

2 T. butter

1 lb. beef top or rib-eye steak, thinly sliced

seasoned salt and pepper to taste

1 onion, sliced

1 clove garlic, minced

Optional: 1 c. sliced mushrooms

1 green pepper, thinly sliced

1 lb. provolone, Gouda or Swiss cheese, sliced

6 hoagie buns or baguettes, split

Melt butter in a skillet over medium heat until slightly browned. Add steak; sprinkle with seasoned salt and pepper and sauté just until browned. Add onion, garlic, mushrooms, if desired, and green pepper; stir. Cover and simmer 5 to 7 minutes or until onion and pepper are tender. Add additional salt and pepper to taste. Remove from heat; set aside. Place 2 to 3 cheese slices in each bun; top each with 2 to 3 tablespoonfuls of steak mixture. Top with additional cheese, if desired. Wrap each sandwich in aluminum foil; bake at 350 degrees for 10 to 15 minutes, until cheese is melted. Makes 6 sandwiches.

Quick tip

Kids will love grilled cheese sandwiches that have been cut out with fun-shaped cookie cutters. Try hearts, shamrocks or even just circles!

Tangy Teriyaki Sandwiches

Kelly Alderson, Erie, PA

1-1/2 lbs. skinless turkey thighs

1/2 c. teriyaki baste and glaze sauce

3 T. orange marmalade

1/4 t. pepper

4 hoagie buns, split

Garnish: sliced green onions

Combine all ingredients except buns and garnish in a slow cooker; cover and cook on low setting for 9 to 10 hours. Remove turkey from slow cooker and shred meat, discarding bones; return to slow cooker. Increase heat to high setting. Cover and cook for 10 to 15 minutes, until sauce is thickened. Serve on hoagie buns. Garnish with green onions. Serves 4.

Susan's Chicken Minis

Susan Brzozowski, Ellicott City, MD

2 T. lemon juice

1/2 c. mayonnaise

salt to taste

1 t. pepper

3-1/2 c. cooked chicken, finely diced

1/2 c. celery, finely diced

1/3 c. raisins

1/3 c. chopped walnuts lettuce leaves

12 mini dinner rolls, split

Combine lemon juice, mayonnaise, salt and pepper in a large bowl. Stir in remaining ingredients except lettuce and rolls. Place lettuce on bottom halves of rolls; top with chicken mixture and top halves of rolls. Makes 12 mini sandwiches.

Susan's Chicken Minis

Tangy Turkey Salad Croissants

Tangy Turkey Salad Croissants

Wendy Jacobs, Idaho Falls, ID

2 c. cooked turkey breast, cubed
1 orange, peeled and chopped
1/2 c. cranberries, finely chopped
1/2 c. mayonnaise
1 t. mustard
1 t. sugar
1/2 t. salt
1/4 c. chopped pecans
6 croissants, split
Garnish: lettuce leaves

Combine turkey, orange, cranberries, mayonnaise, mustard, sugar and salt; chill. Stir in pecans before serving. Top each croissant half with 1/2 cup turkey mixture and a lettuce leaf. Top with remaining croissant half. Makes 6 sandwiches.

Italian Meatball Subs

Italian Meatball Subs

Dana Thompson, Prospect, OH

1 onion, sliced
1/2 c. green pepper, sliced
2 T. water
8-oz. can pizza sauce
24 meatballs, cooked
4 Italian hard rolls, sliced and hollowed out
1/2 c. shredded provolone cheese

Cook onion, pepper and water, covered, in a large saucepan over medium heat just until tender; drain. Stir in pizza sauce and meatballs; cook until hot and bubbly. Fill each roll with 6 meatballs; top with sauce. Sprinkle with cheese and add roll tops. Place sandwiches in a lightly greased 13"x9" baking pan. Bake at 400 degrees for 10 to 15 minutes or until bread is crusty and cheese is melted. Makes 4 sandwiches.

Ranch Chicken Wraps

Lea Ann Burwell, Charles Town, WV

1/2 t. oil
4 boneless, skinless chicken breasts, cut into strips
2.8-oz. can French-fried onions
1/4 c. bacon bits
8-oz. pkg. shredded Cheddar cheese
lettuce leaves
8 to 10 8-inch flour tortillas
Garnish: ranch salad dressing

Heat oil in a large non-stick skillet over medium heat. Add chicken and cook until golden and juices run clear when chicken is pierced. Add onions, bacon bits and cheese to skillet; cook until cheese melts. Place several lettuce leaves on each tortilla and spoon chicken mixture down center; roll up. Serve with ranch salad dressing. Makes 8 to 10 wraps.

Sandwiches

Tailgate Sandwich Ring
Crystal Vogel, Springdale, PA

2 11-oz. tubes refrigerated
   French bread dough
1/2 lb. bacon, crisply
   cooked and crumbled
3/4 c. mayonnaise
1 T. green onions, chopped

1/2 lb. deli sliced turkey
1/2 lb. deli sliced ham
1/2 lb. sliced provolone
   cheese
2 tomatoes, sliced
2 c. lettuce, chopped

Spray a Bundt® pan with non-stick vegetable spray.
Place both tubes of dough into pan, seam-side up,
joining ends together to form one large ring. Pinch
edges to seal tightly. Lightly spray top of dough with
non-stick vegetable spray. Bake at 350 degrees for 40
to 45 minutes, until golden. Carefully turn out; cool
completely. Combine bacon, mayonnaise and onions;
mix well. Slice bread horizontally. Spread half the bacon
mixture over bottom half of bread. Top with turkey, ham
and provolone. Place on an ungreased baking sheet.
Bake at 350 degrees for 5 minutes, or until cheese melts.
Top with tomatoes and lettuce. Spread remaining bacon
mixture on top half of bread; place over lettuce. Slice
into wedges. Serves 8.

Quick tip
Tuck burgers into halved pita pockets...easy
for small hands to hold and a tasty change
from regular hamburger buns.

Shortcut Stromboli

Shortcut Stromboli
Becky Kuchenbecker, Ravenna, OH

1 loaf frozen bread dough,
   thawed
1 T. grated Parmesan
   cheese
2 eggs, separated
2 T. oil
1 t. dried parsley

1 t. dried oregano
1/2 t. garlic powder
1/2 lb. deli ham, sliced✓
1/4 lb. deli salami, sliced✓
6-oz. pkg. shredded ✓
   Cheddar cheese

Spread thawed dough in a rectangle on a greased
baking sheet. Mix Parmesan cheese, egg yolks, oil and
seasonings in a bowl. Spread Parmesan cheese mixture
on top of dough. Layer with meat and Cheddar cheese.
Roll up jelly-roll style; place seam-side down on baking
sheet. Let rise about 20 minutes. Brush with egg whites.
Bake, uncovered, at 350 degrees for 30 to 40 minutes,
until golden. Slice to serve. Serves 6.

Tailgate Sandwich Ring

Mexican Hot Dogs
Leslie Limon, Yahualica, Mexico

8 hot dogs
8 slices bacon
8 hot dog buns
1 c. sour cream
1/2 c. onion, chopped
3/4 c. tomato, chopped
4-oz. can chopped jalapeño peppers, drained
Garnish: mustard and catsup

Pierce hot dogs with a fork 3 or 4 times. Wrap one slice of bacon around each hot dog. Over medium heat, grill or sauté on a griddle until bacon is lightly golden on all sides. Remove wire twist from hot dog bun bag. Microwave buns in bag for 30 to 45 seconds. Carefully remove buns from bag; cut open buns. Spread sour cream on both halves of each bun. Place bacon-wrapped hot dog in bun. Top with onion, tomato and jalapeños. Garnish with mustard and catsup. Makes 8.

> ✳ ### Quick tip
>
> Mini burgers are fun for dinner...perfect for parties too, since everyone can take just what they want! Look for slider buns at the grocery store, or use mini brown & serve rolls for buns.

Sweet & Sauerkraut Brats
Jo Ann

1-1/2 to 2 lbs. bratwurst, cut into bite-size pieces
27-oz. can sauerkraut
4 tart apples, peeled, cored and chopped
1/4 c. onion, chopped
1/4 c. brown sugar, packed
1 t. caraway seed
4 to 6 hard rolls, split
Garnish: spicy mustard

Place bratwurst in a 5 to 6-quart slow cooker. Toss together undrained sauerkraut, apples, onion, brown sugar and caraway seed; spoon over bratwurst. Cover and cook on high setting one hour; reduce heat to low setting and cook 2 to 3 more hours, stirring occasionally. Fill rolls, using a slotted spoon. Serve with mustard on the side, if desired. Serves 4 to 6.

Mini Turkey-Berry Bites
Jackie Smulski, Lyons, IL

2 c. biscuit baking mix
1/2 c. sweetened dried cranberries
1 c. milk
2 T. Dijon mustard
1 egg, beaten
6-oz. pkg. thinly sliced smoked turkey, chopped and divided
3/4 c. shredded Swiss cheese, divided

Stir together baking mix, cranberries, milk, mustard and egg until blended. Pour half the batter into a lightly greased 8"x8" baking pan. Arrange half the turkey over batter; sprinkle half the cheese nearly to edges of pan. Top with remaining turkey, followed by remaining batter. Bake, uncovered, at 350 degrees for 45 to 50 minutes, until golden and set. Sprinkle with remaining cheese; let stand 5 minutes. To serve, cut into 9 squares; slice each square diagonally. Makes 1-1/2 dozen.

Mexican Hot Dogs

Papa's Italian Sandwiches

Papa's Italian Sandwiches

Geneva Rogers, Gillette, WY

24 Italian pork sausage
   links
5 green peppers, thinly
   sliced
1 onion, chopped
12-oz. can tomato paste
15-oz. can tomato sauce
1 c. water
1 T. sugar

5 cloves garlic, minced
1-1/4 t. dried oregano
1 t. dried basil
1 t. salt
24 hoagie rolls, split
Garnish: grated Parmesan
   cheese

Brown 6 to 8 sausages at a time in a large Dutch oven
over medium heat. Drain sausages and set aside,
reserving 3 tablespoons drippings in Dutch oven. Add
peppers and onion. Sauté until crisp-tender; drain. Stir
in tomato paste, tomato sauce, water, sugar, garlic, herbs
and salt. Add sausages; bring to a boil over medium heat.
Reduce heat; simmer, covered, 30 to 45 minutes. Serve
on rolls; sprinkle with cheese. Makes 24 servings.

Potluck Beef Sandwiches

Potluck Beef Sandwiches

Carmen Chandler, Roseburg, OR

1 lb. ground beef
1/4 onion, chopped
salt and pepper to taste
2/3 c. barbecue sauce
2 8-oz. tubes refrigerated
   crescent rolls

1/2 to 1 c. shredded
   Cheddar cheese
Garnish: additional
   barbecue sauce

In a skillet over medium heat, brown beef and onion.
Add a little salt and pepper; drain. Mix in barbecue
sauce. Place crescent rolls on a baking sheet and make
a rectangle, pinching seams together. Spoon beef
mixture down center of dough and sprinkle with cheese.
Fold the sides over and seal dough down the center.
Bake at 375 degrees for 20 minutes, or until golden. Slice
into portions and serve with additional barbecue sauce.
Serves 4.

*Quick tip

Toast hamburger buns or sandwich rolls
before spooning on juicy fillings...buns won't
get soggy!

Mama's Quick Meatball Subs 🍴

Cris Goode, Mooresville, IN

1 lb. extra-lean ground beef

20 saltine crackers, crushed

12-oz. bottle chili sauce, divided

1/4 c. grated Parmesan cheese

2 egg whites, beaten

salt and pepper to taste

15-oz. jar pizza sauce, warmed

2 loaves French baguettes, halved and split

2 cups favorite shredded cheese

Combine beef, cracker crumbs, half of chili sauce, Parmesan cheese, egg whites, salt and pepper in a bowl. Mix well; form into 16, 1-1/2 inch meatballs. Place on a baking sheet sprayed with non-stick vegetable spray. Bake at 400 degrees for 15 minutes, or until golden, turning meatballs halfway through. Add baked meatballs to warmed sauce. Fill each half-loaf with 4 meatballs and sprinkle with cheese. Serve with remaining chili sauce on the side. Serves 4.

Quick tip

Be creative with everyone's favorite, grilled cheese...try sourdough, Italian, rye or egg bread as well as good ol' white bread!

PB & Berries

PB & Berries 🍴 p. 260

Jo Ann

1 T. creamy peanut butter

3 slices whole-wheat bread

1 T. whipped cream cheese

2 strawberries, hulled and sliced

1 t. honey

Spread peanut butter on one slice of bread; arrange strawberries on top and drizzle with honey. Place a plain piece of bread on top of peanut butter slice. Spread cream cheese on remaining slice of bread and place on top. Cut into halves. Makes 2 servings.

Banana Bread

Mama's Quick Meatball Subs

Kentucky Hot Browns

Kentucky Hot Browns

Angie Stone, Argillite, KY

1/4 c. butter
1/4 c. all-purpose flour
2 c. milk
2 cubes chicken bouillon
16-oz. pkg. pasteurized process cheese spread, cubed

6 slices bread, toasted
12 slices deli turkey
6 slices deli ham
6 slices bacon, crisply cooked
6 slices tomato

Melt butter in a heavy saucepan over low heat. Stir in flour until smooth. Cook one minute, stirring constantly. Stir in milk and bouillon cubes. Cook until thick and bubbly. Add cheese and stir until smooth. Place toast slices in a buttered 13"x9" baking pan. Layer each with turkey and ham. Evenly spread cheese sauce over ham. Top each with bacon and tomato. Bake, uncovered, at 350 degrees for 3 to 5 minutes, until bubbly. Makes 6 servings.

Dressed-Up Dogs

Shawna Weathers, Judsonia, AR

8 hot dogs
8 slices rye bread, toasted
mayonnaise-type salad dressing to taste
2 kosher dill pickles, each cut lengthwise into 4 slices

4 slices Swiss cheese
Optional: mustard to taste

Slice hot dogs lengthwise, taking care not to cut all the way through. Place hot dogs cut-side down on a lightly greased hot griddle. Cook on each side until golden and heated through; set aside. Spread 4 slices bread with salad dressing; top each with 2 pickle slices, 2 hot dogs and one slice cheese. Spread remaining 4 slices bread with mustard, if using. Place on top of sandwiches. Makes 4 sandwiches.

Texas Steak Sandwiches

Julie Horn, Chrisney, IN

8 slices frozen Texas toast
1-1/2 lbs. deli roast beef, sliced
steak sauce to taste

16 slices provolone cheese
Optional: sautéed green pepper

Place Texas toast on an ungreased baking sheet. Bake at 425 degrees for 5 minutes per side, or until softened and lightly golden; set aside. Warm roast beef in a skillet over medium heat until most of juice has evaporated; stir in steak sauce. Place one cheese slice on each toast slice. Divide beef evenly among toast slices; top with remaining 8 cheese slices and, if desired, sautéed green pepper and onion slices. Place beef-topped toast on an ungreased baking sheet; bake at 425 degrees until cheese melts. Makes 8 open-faced sandwiches.

Quick tip

Many's the long night I've dreamed of cheese…toasted, mostly.
-Robert Louis Stevenson

Hearty Chicken-Bacon Melts

Hearty Chicken-Bacon Melts •
Vickie

4 boneless, skinless
  chicken breasts

1 onion, sliced

2 t. margarine

2 t. olive oil

4 slices bread, toasted

4 t. steak sauce

8 slices bacon, crisply
  cooked

1 c. shredded Cheddar
  cheese

Place chicken between pieces of wax paper and flatten
to about 1/4-inch thickness. In a large skillet, cook onion
in margarine and oil until softened. Remove onion
from skillet. Add chicken to skillet; cook for about 7
to 9 minutes on each side, until cooked through. Place
toasted bread slices on a large baking sheet; spread each
slice with one teaspoon steak sauce. Top each with a
chicken breast, 2 slices bacon, 1/4 of onion slices and
1/4 cup cheese. Broil 4 to 6 inches from heat for one to 2
minutes, until cheese is melted. Serves 4.

Grilled Salmon BLTs
Edie DeSpain, Logan, UT

1/3 c. mayonnaise

2 t. fresh dill, chopped

1 t. lemon zest

4 1-inch thick salmon
  fillets

1/4 t. salt

1/8 t. pepper

8 1/2-inch thick slices
  country-style bread

4 romaine lettuce leaves

2 tomatoes, sliced

6 slices bacon, crisply
  cooked and halved

Stir together mayonnaise, dill and zest in a small bowl;
set aside. Sprinkle salmon with salt and pepper; place
on a lightly greased hot grill, skin-side down. Cover and
cook over medium heat about 10 to 12 minutes, without
turning, until cooked through. Slide a thin metal spatula
between salmon and skin; lift salmon and transfer to a
plate. Discard skin. Arrange bread slices on grill; cook
until lightly toasted on both sides. Spread mayonnaise
mixture on one side of 4 bread slices. Top each bread
slice with one lettuce leaf, 2 tomato slices, 3 half-slices
bacon, one salmon fillet and remaining bread slice.
Makes 4 sandwiches.

✳ Quick tip

Lighten up your old favorite, grilled cheese…
spritz the bread with a little butter-flavored
non-stick vegetable spray before grilling,
instead of spreading with butter. You'll enjoy
all the flavor without the calories.

Grilled Salmon BLTs

INDEX

INDEX

Sandwiches

INDEX

Savory Biscuits, Rolls & Crackers

Savory Breads

INDEX

Send us your favorite recipe

...and the memory that makes it special for you!

If we select your recipe for a brand-new **Gooseberry Patch** cookbook, your name will appear right along with it...and you'll receive a FREE copy of the book!

Submit your recipe on our website at www.gooseberrypatch.com/sharearecipe or mail to: Gooseberry Patch, PO Box 812, Columbus, OH 43216

*Please include the number of servings and all other necessary information.

Have a taste for more?

Visit www.gooseberrypatch.com to join our Circle of Friends!
- Free recipes, tips and ideas plus a complete cookbook index
- Get special email offers and our monthly eLetter delivered to your inbox